Cambridge Proficiency
Examination Practice 3

Cambridge Proficiency

Examination Practice 3

University of Cambridge
Local Examinations Syndicate

CAMBRIDGE
UNIVERSITY PRESS

PUBLISHED BY THE PRESS SYNDICATE OF THE UNIVERSITY OF CAMBRIDGE
The Pitt Building, Trumpington Street, Cambridge CB2 1RP, United Kingdom

CAMBRIDGE UNIVERSITY PRESS
The Edinburgh Building, Cambridge CB2 2RU, United Kingdom
40 West 20th Street, New York, NY 10011–4211, USA
10 Stamford Road, Oakleigh, Melbourne 3166, Australia

First published 1989
Seventh printing 1997

Printed in the United Kingdom at the University Press, Cambridge

ISBN 0 521 36777 8 Student's Book
ISBN 0 521 36778 6 Teacher's Book
ISBN 0 521 36600 3 Class Cassette Set

Contents

To the student

This book is for candidates preparing for the University of Cambridge Certificate of Proficiency in English examination and provides practice in all the written and oral papers. It contains 5 complete tests, based on the Proficiency examinations set in 1986 and 1987, and incorporates the modifications made to Paper 5 (the Interview) in December 1985. The examination consists of 5 papers, as follows:

Paper 1 Reading Comprehension (1 hour)
Section A consists of 25 multiple-choice items in the form of a sentence with a blank to be filled by 1 of 4 words or phrases.
Section B consists of 15 multiple-choice items based on 2 or more reading passages of different types.

Paper 2 Composition (2 hours)
There are 5 topics from which you choose 2. The topics include discursive, descriptive and narrative essays, a directed writing exercise and an essay based on optional reading. (In these practice tests the questions based on optional reading are set on the kind of books that are prescribed each year. These are *not* the actual books prescribed for any particular year: they are just given as examples.)

Paper 3 Use of English (2 hours)
Section A contains exercises of various kinds which test your control of English usage and grammatical structure.
Section B consists of a passage followed by questions which test your comprehension and skill in summarising.

Paper 4 Listening Comprehension (about 30 minutes)
You answer a variety of questions on 3 or 4 recorded passages from English broadcasts, interviews, announcements, phone messages and conversations. Each passage is heard twice.

Paper 5 Interview (15 to 20 minutes)
You take part in a conversation based on a photograph, passage and other material from authentic sources linked by theme, either with a group of other candidates or with the examiner alone. The exercises in these tests include some of the type set in the examination on optional reading.

Practice Test 1

PAPER 1 READING COMPREHENSION   (1 hour)

Answer all questions. Indicate your choice of answer in every case **on the separate answer sheet** *already given out, which should show your name and examination index number. Follow carefully the instructions about how to record your answers. Give* **one answer only** *to each question. Marks will not be deducted for wrong answers: your total score on this test will be the number of correct answers you give.*

SECTION A

In this section you must choose the word or phrase which best completes each sentence. **On your answer sheet** *indicate the letter A, B, C, or D against the number of each item 1 to 25 for the word or phrase you choose.*

1 He told his father a long and .... story to explain his lateness.
   A inconceivable   B unconvincing   C unimaginable   D incredulous

2 He .... me to believe that they had left the district.
   A made   B led   C assured   D confirmed

3 We sat on after the meal, ... the taste of the fine brandy.
   A indulging   B sensing   C sipping   D savouring

4 That minister's .... of party politics is well known to the public.
   A disgust   B objection   C dislike   D opposition

5 At school he had a good academic record, and also .... at sports.
   A prevailed   B achieved   C surpassed   D excelled

6 But .... some countries have ruined their agriculture, squandering money on uneconomic factories, the Ivory Coast has stuck to what it is good at.
   A after   B during   C when   D while

7 Old houses have a .... to be draughty.
   A tendency   B habit   C problem   D characteristic

8 He lost his job .... no fault of his own.
   A through   B by   C with   D over

9   He was completely .... by her tale of hardship.
    A taken away   B taken down   C taken in   D taken up

10 The lecture was rather boring, but the .... discussion proved
    fruitful.
    A subsequent   B latter   C consecutive   D successive

11 After leaving school, Nigel decided to .... in the army.
    A enlist   B enrol   C register   D sign

12 The painting was a valuable family possession, which had been
    .... from generation to generation.
    A handed over   B handed down   C handed out   D handed across

13 By an unfortunate ...., the bride's sister was not invited to the
    wedding.
    A insult   B oversight   C neglect   D disregard

14 .... a fire, hotel guests are asked to remain calm.
    A As a result of   B In the event of   C By reason of   D In the time of

15 When I went into the dining room next morning, the .... of the
    dinner were still on the table.
    A remains   B results   C remnants   D relics

16 There's a tiny .... in the diamond; that's why the ring is so cheap.
    A deformity   B error   C flaw   D scar

17 Too many hotels have been built and this has .... down prices,
    making holidays cheaper.
    A forced   B cut   C slowed   D reduced

18 Because of the shortage of water there is a .... on the use of
    hose-pipes.
    A ban   B veto   C taboo   D boycott

19 She can't be interested in the lessons, ... that she always arrives
    late.
    A viewing   B seeing   C noting   D judging

20 When his business failed, he started again from ....
    A scratch   B blank   C introduction   D beginning

21 The lecture .... from prehistory to modern times and gave the
    audience much to think about.
    A covered   B included   C ranged   D dealt   ⟫▶

22 I will keep your application .... file for the time being.
   A in   B with   C on   D at

23 It's a foregone .... that he'll be top of the class again.
   A concept   B proposal   C conclusion   D prediction

24 The number of tickets available will be .... by the size of the stadium.
   A related   B determined   C dependent   D consequent

25 After the accident, traffic had to be .... away from the motorway.
   A diverted   B deflected   C dispersed   D disposed

SECTION B

In this section you will find after each of the passages a number of questions or unfinished statements about the passage, each with four suggested answers or ways of finishing. You must choose the one which you think fits best according to the passage. **On your answer sheet ,** *indicate the letter A, B, C or D against the number of each item 26–40 for the answer you choose. Give* **one answer only** *to each question. Read each passage right through before choosing your answers.*

FIRST PASSAGE

Cordelia said: 'Someone told me about the theatre. The present owner must be rich. It can't have been cheap, restoring the theatre and the castle and collecting the Victorian antiques.'

It was Miss Maudsley who replied: 'Oh, but he is! He made a fortune out of that bestseller he wrote, *Autopsy*. He's A. K. Ambrose. Didn't you know?'

Cordelia hadn't known. She had bought the paperback, as had thousands of others, because she had got tired of seeing its dramatic cover confronting her in every bookshop and supermarket. She had felt curious to know what it was about a first novel that could earn a reputed half a million before publication. It was fashionably long and equally fashionably violent and she remembered that she had indeed, as the advertisement promised, found it difficult to put down, without now being able to remember clearly either the plot or the characters. The idea had been neat enough. The novel dealt with an inquest on a murder victim and had told at length the stories of all the people involved, police surgeon, detective inspector, family of the victim, victim and, finally, the murderer. You could, she supposed, call it a crime novel with a difference, the difference being that there had been more sex than detection and that the book had attempted with some success to combine the popular family saga with the mystery. The writing style had been nicely judged for the mass market, neither good enough to spoil its popular appeal nor bad enough to make people ashamed of being seen reading it in public. At the end she had been left dis-satisfied, but whether that was because she had felt manipulated or because of a conviction that A. K. Ambrose could have written a better book had he chosen, it was hard to say.

Miss Maudsley was anxious to disclaim any implied criticism in her ques-tion. 'It's not surprising you didn't know. I wouldn't have known myself, only one of the members on our club outing has a husband who keeps a bookshop and she told us. Mr Ambrose doesn't really like it to be known. It's the only book he's written, I believe.'

26 Cordelia bought the book because
   A   everybody else was buying it.
   B   it was easy to get hold of.
   C   she wanted to know what was special about it.
   D   she was fascinated by the subject.

27 What lasting impression did the book make on Cordelia?
   A   It was a clever idea but badly handled.
   B   It was enjoyable but easy to forget.
   C   It had too many detailed descriptions of people.
   D   It was too long and too violent.

28 What characterized the style of the book?
   A   It was not literary enough.
   B   It was too highbrow for most tastes.
   C   It was undemanding and readable.
   D   It was embarrassingly badly written.

29 Why was Miss Maudsley worried about her question?
   A   She thought she might have seemed rude.
   B   She was afraid she had given away a secret.
   C   She wasn't sure of her facts.
   D   She thought Cordelia hadn't understood what she meant.

SECOND PASSAGE

I must warn you that you may find parts of this article rather difficult to under-stand. Wait! The sentence you have just read is quite untrue. But that isn't why you were irritated by it. It was, of course, also insulting and few people enjoy being insulted. By reading this article you are making the claim that you are the sort of person who will understand it; my opening sentence questioned your claim, and that is what made it insulting. In other words, an insult occurs whenever one person denies some aspect of identity which another is claiming, explicitly or otherwise.

[5]

When describing the course of a disease, pathologists often talk of the body organising its defences in response to a biological insult. But in everyday life we use the term only when the rules which govern social encounters are breached in the manner described. For social interaction to work it is essential that the participants respect the 'face' of all involved. 'Face' refers to the public image which a person chooses to present in a particular situation. Its importance is obvious when two people are talking to each other, but it cannot be ignored by the writer who wishes to keep his readers.

If I wish to insult you, I must not merely threaten your face, but do so deliberately. Without malicious intent, I am guilty of a social blunder but nothing worse. Some people are famous for dropping bricks, but they are considered socially unskilled or naive rather than insulting; this can be seen from the fact that their remarks elicit laughter, admittedly strained, rather than anger.

What happens when face is lost? It is usually possible to avoid or overlook the insult ('I didn't hear that' / 'She's only a child'). If it is not overlooked, the next move is conventionally a challenge in which the victim draws attention to the violation ('What do you mean, I've got the manners of a pig?'). This is an invitation to the offender to restore order by making a response which indicates that the conventions have not after all been violated. He may apologise ('I don't know what came over me') or make compensation ('I'm always throwing my food all over the place'). Alternatively, he can attempt to change the meaning of his remark ('I was only joking' / 'I can't stand people who eat delicately'). Any of these ploys can repair the damage, so long as the wounded party accepts the explanation and the offender confirms his penitence by a display of suitable gratitude.

30 What is the author's intention in the opening sentence of this passage?
   A   to prepare the reader for difficulties
   B   to make the article appear very impressive
   C   to discourage uneducated readers
   D   to demonstrate the nature of an insult

31 The author suggests that an insult is an attack on another person's
   A   image of himself.
   B   good character.
   C   standard of intelligence.
   D   ability to understand himself.

32 According to the passage, why is it important for 'face' to be respected?
   A   so that people can talk freely to each other
   B   to allow the adoption of new roles
   C   to maintain an acceptable pattern of behaviour
   D   so that people can understand one another better

[6]

33 People who are 'famous for dropping bricks'
    A   are unintentionally rude.
    B   cannot control their behaviour.
    C   are trying to be funny.
    D   do not care what others think of them.

34 An insult will normally be challenged
    A   when it is very obvious.
    B   to allow it to be withdrawn.
    C   to allow the victim to retaliate.
    D   if the offender was only joking.

35 'Face' can only be restored when
    A   the victim learns to laugh at himself.
    B   the offender also receives an insult.
    C   the victim accepts the truth of the insult.
    D   the offender appears thankful for forgiveness.

THIRD PASSAGE

The potential of computers for increasing the control of organisations or society over their members and for invading the privacy of those members has caused considerable concern.

The privacy issue has been raised most insistently with respect to the creation and maintenance of data files that assemble information about persons from a multitude of sources. Files of this kind would be highly valuable for many kinds of economic and social research, but they are bought at too high a price if they endanger human freedom or seriously enhance the opportunities of blackmailers. While such dangers should not be ignored, it should be noted that the lack of comprehensive data files has never before been the limiting barrier to the suppression of human freedom.

Making the computer the villain in the invasion of privacy or encroachment on civil liberties simply diverts attention from the real dangers. Computer data banks can and must be given the highest degree of protection from abuse. But we must be careful, also, that we do not employ such crude methods of protection as to deprive our society of important data it needs to understand its own social processes and to analyse its problems.

Perhaps the most important question of all about the computer is what it has done and will do to man's view of himself and his place in the universe. The most heated attacks on the computer are not focused on its possible economic effects, its presumed destruction of job satisfaction, or its threat to privacy and liberty, but upon the claim that it causes people to be viewed, and to view themselves, as 'machines'.

What the computer and the progress in artificial intelligence challenge is an ethic that rests on man's apartness from the rest of nature. An alternative ethic,

[7]

of course, views man as a part of nature, governed by natural law, subject to the forces of gravity and the demands of his body. The debate about artificial intelligence and the simulation of man's thinking is, in considerable part, a confrontation of these two views of man's place in the universe.

36   Why is it important to prevent the abuse of computer data banks?
    A   to protect the rights of the individual
    B   to maintain discipline in society
    C   to encourage economic and social research
    D   to collect wide-ranging information

37   Too much caution in the use of computers will
    A   prevent the solution of economic problems.
    B   cause more suppression of human freedom.
    C   lead to clumsy methods of protection.
    D   interfere with our study of society.

38   What lessons can be learned from the past in this debate?
    A   Crime has always been associated with progress.
    B   Attacks on freedom are nothing new.
    C   The accumulation of data encourages oppression.
    D   Privacy has been a neglected issue.

39   The arrival of the computer has made man
    A   have more difficulty understanding himself.
    B   think more like a machine.
    C   look at himself in a different way.
    D   gain less satisfaction from his work.

40   If you had to split this passage into two sections, where would be the best place to make the division?
    A   after the first paragraph
    B   after the second paragraph
    C   after the third paragraph
    D   after the fourth paragraph

PAPER 2   COMPOSITION   (2 hours)

*Write **two only** of the following composition exercises. Your answers must follow exactly the instructions given. Write in pen, not pencil. You are allowed to make alterations, but see that your work is clear and easy to read.*

1   Describe how you would entertain a weekend visitor to your home. (About 350 words)

2   'Works of art and archaeological treasures should remain in their country of origin.' Discuss. (About 350 words)

3   Write the story of the 'most unloved person who ever lived' (About 350 words)

4   A motorway is to be built. Two routes have been proposed as shown on the map, one through an area of outstanding natural beauty, the other through the residential outskirts of a small market town. At the enquiry, the local conservationists and the residents of the town argue in support of their chosen route. Write **two** speeches (about 150 words for each) expressing each point of view.

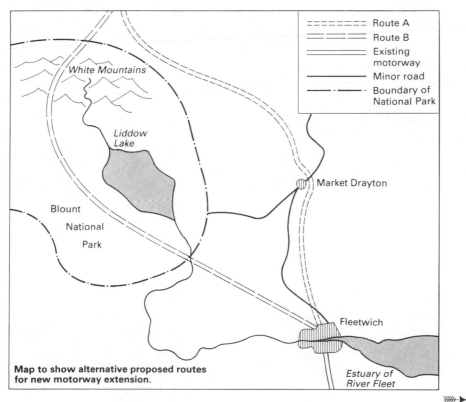

Map to show alternative proposed routes for new motorway extension.

5   Basing your answer on your reading of the prescribed text concerned,
    answer *one* of the following. (About 350 words)

PATRICIA HIGHSMITH: *The Talented Mr Ripley*
To what extent does Tom Ripley's love of travelling cause him to commit
murder?

JOHN OSBORNE: *The Entertainer*
'I'm dead behind the eyes.' Explain Archie Rice's comment about himself
and say how far you agree with it.

D. H. LAWRENCE: *Selected Tales*
'One thing which Lawrence really understands is the suffering in women's
lives.' Discuss how true you think this statement is, in relation to two or
three of the stories.

PAPER 3 USE OF ENGLISH (2 hours)

SECTION A

1 *Fill each of the numbered blanks in the following passage with* **one** *suitable word.*

The essence of chemistry consists of the making of new substances, and a chemical change is defined .... (1) the changing of one substance .... (2) another. Many .... (3) chemical changes have been performed by man .... (4) very early times, probably the .... (5) being the heating of clay to make pottery, which has been known for 10,000 years. Even .... (6) this, of course, man had discovered fire – another .... (7) change – but here the importance of the reaction lies in the heat-energy produced .... (8) than in the ashes, smoke and gases, which are the final products.

Progress .... (9) chemistry was .... (10) because of the absence of any adequate theory to explain these changes, and because the earliest theory ('alchemy') was so blindly optimistic .... (11) to assume that .... (12) could be changed into anything else. In particular, the alchemists thought that they could change a base metal .... (13) lead into gold and so get rich quickly. Not until .... (14) than 200 years ago were the true foundations of chemistry .... (15) by painstaking researches .... (16) the nature of air and water, in fact by pure disinterested curiosity, allied to the habit of mind which takes nothing for .... (17). Chemists learned that before they could make new substances they must .... (18) discover what ordinary things are made .... (19); in technical language, analysis must always .... (20) synthesis.

2 *Finish each of the following sentences in such a way that it means exactly the same as the sentence printed before it.*

> EXAMPLE: Immediately after his arrival things went wrong.
>
> ANSWER: No sooner *had he arrived than things went wrong.*

a) It's such a pity your sister can't come as well.

If only ....

b) The house seemed to have been unoccupied for several months.

It looked ....

c) These new machines have put an end to queuing.

Before these ....

d) He was so tired he fell asleep before the end of the film.

He was too ....

e) Though my house was cheaper than Norman's, it is bigger and more attractive.

Norman's house may ....

f) Everyone heard about the accident before I did.

I was the ....

g) 'If you must go out tonight, at least finish your homework first!' said Sarah's father.

Sarah's father said that if ....

h) The instructions say you just add boiling water to the soup powder.

The soup powder ....

3   *Fill each of the blanks with a suitable word or phrase.*

EXAMPLE: Even if I had stood on a chair, *I wouldn't have been able to* reach the light bulb.

a)   Only when he removed his dark glasses ....

.... who he was.

b)   Let's go home. There's .... waiting any

longer.

c)   After having had a chauffeur for so many years my brother took some

time to .... himself.

d)   If you had really wanted to succeed, you ....

.... time on your studies and less on playing games.

e)   The more driving practice you have, the better chance you ....

.... your test.

f)   He doesn't mind one way or the other; it makes ....

.... him.

4   *For each of the sentences below, write a new sentence* **as similar as possible in meaning to the original sentence,** *but using the word given. This word must* **not be altered** *in any way.*

> EXAMPLE: Not many people attended the meeting.
> **turnout**

> ANSWER: *There was a poor turnout for the meeting.*

a)   Be sure to say goodbye to your grandmother before you leave.
without

....

b)   That sort of behaviour is deplorable, in my opinion.
approve

....

c)   The new lecturer was unpopular with his students.
take

....

d)   The last political scandal of this kind took place fifty years ago.
since

....

e)   Women are not allowed to enter the inner temple.
let

....

f)   They'll have to take the dog on holiday with them.
behind

....

g)   Don't run away with the idea that this job is easy.
conclusion

....

h)   You must drive more slowly in town.
reduce

....

[14]

SECTION B

5   *Read the following passage, then answer the questions which follow it.*

Few people can irritate like recent converts, whether to religion, a word-
processor or Health; until recently, I would have put the born-again non-
smoker high on my list of Pests Best Avoided.

Can't they, I felt, be content just smugly not to die of lung cancer
themselves, without going round ostentatiously opening windows and   5
giving on-the-spot lectures? No one who has not been living down a disused mineshaft for the past 20 years can fail to know that smoking is bad
for you, so anyone who does smoke presumably has their reasons; can't
they be left alone?

Oh, but being smoked at is almost as bad for you as smoking, we're   10
now told. Possibly, but what about all the other nuisances – people who
cough their colds in your face, for instance? It seemed to me a simple
civil liberties issue: live and let live. But I'm increasingly seeing these
tiresome crusaders in a different light. I see them not so much as people
who bully the individual, but as puny Davids in a fight where the   15
tobacco Goliaths have it far too much their own way.

Sport depends heavily on tobacco sponsorship, while papers and
magazines couldn't do without its advertising. The cigarette firms say,
'We aren't aiming at the young. What a suggestion!' However, since
they kill off 100,000 of their customers every year, they obviously have to   20
recruit new talent somewhere.

The British Medical Association and dozens of health and youth
bodies recently petitioned the Government to put up taxes on cigarettes,
and it might well do so – but the more it's dependent on tobacco tax for
revenue, the less it is actually going to do anything to curb the industry.   25
Indeed, it positively encourages it. The Health Promotion Research Trust
is a smokescreen body set up by the tobacco trade to research everything
but the effects of tobacco. When the Government's own Health Education Council recently crossed swords with it, it was they – not the HPRT
– that were rapped over the knuckles by Whitehall.   30

What could be done? At least people needn't unwittingly help the
tobacco trade along. Last year the BMA published a shock horror list of
worthies – charities, trusts, Lords, colleges, even health authorities –
which held tobacco-related shares, and quite a few of them did sell out.

What about education? I'm not too hopeful, if only because my own   35
sons went without pause from lecturing their father on the evils of the
weed to being smokers themselves; under the influence, it seems, of
peer group pressure. But there is one sort of peer group pressure, it
occurs to me, which doesn't happen at all. In other spheres, we come
down much harder on the pusher than the addict, on the pimp than the   40
prostitute (let alone her client). Grand Met, the hotel combine, nearly
did pull out of tobacco a while ago, but changed their minds; might the

[15]

decision not have gone the other way if the directors' own pals had been saying: 'Well, yes, I know old boy. We all have to make money, of course. Only – isn't it rather a smelly business to be in?'.   45

a) What is meant by the expression 'born-again non-smoker' (lines 2–3)? ......

    ....

b) What is the purpose of the reference to someone 'living down a disused mineshaft' (lines 6–7)?

    ....

    ....

c) Explain in your own words 'being smoked at' (line 10) ....

    ....

d) Who are the people referred to as 'these tiresome crusaders' (lines 13–14) and how has the writer's opinion of them changed recently?

    ....

    ....

    ....

e) Who are the 'tobacco Goliaths' and in what sense are they 'having it far too much their own way' (line 16)?

    ....

    ....

    ....

f) What is meant by 'recruit new talent' (line 21) and what point is the writer making here?

    ....

    ....

    ....

g) What is the meaning of the word 'smokescreen' in line 27?

....

....

h) Give another expression for 'rapped over the knuckles' (line 30).

....

....

i) Who are the people who 'unwittingly help the tobacco trade along' (lines 31–32)?

....

....

j) How did the 'peer group pressure' mentioned in line 38 affect the writer's children?

....

....

k) What is the relevance of the example of the 'pusher' and the 'addict' (line 40)?

....

....

l) What is meant by 'Grand Met . . . nearly did pull out of tobacco' (lines 41–42)?

....

....

m) How could peer group pressure reduce support for the tobacco companies?

....

.... ⟫►

[17]

n) In a paragraph of 60 to 80 words, summarise the difficulties which, according to the writer, stand in the way of a campaign against cigarettes, and state briefly her proposals for a solution.

....

....

....

....

....

....

....

....

....

....

....

PAPER 4 LISTENING COMPREHENSION
(about 30 minutes)

FIRST PART

Listen to the County World radio programme on a village called Mickleham. Look at the notes made by the interviewer and for questions 1–13 fill in the missing information in the spaces provided by writing **brief** *answers. You are given two examples of what to write.*

<u>Programme</u>:   County World
         The Village of Mickleham
         Interviews with Mrs Mo Chisman
         and Mrs Gwynne Anderson

Day of broadcast: (**1**) ....

Questions to put to

* <u>Mrs Mo Chisman</u>

  Where is Mickleham? on the Old London Road
  Age of Church? (**2**) ....
  How long has Mo lived there? 30 years
  How long has Mo's husband lived there? (**3**) ....
  When has the village changed most? (**4**) ....
  Why are there no new buildings? (**5**) ....

* <u>Mrs Gwynne Anderson</u>

  What is her position at the local school? (**6**) ....
  In which year did she start working in Mickleham? (**7**) ....
  How does she feel about working there? (**8**) ....

[19]

Is the population of Mickleham growing? ⑨ ....

In which year was the first school in Mickleham founded? ⑩ ....

* <u>Future events in Mickleham</u>

             Two events in October   ⑪ ....

                                  ⑫ ....

        Date of horticultural show ⑬ ....

SECOND PART

Listen to the interview with Trevor MacDonald, chosen as 'tie-man of the year'.
For each of the questions 14–17 tick (✓) one of the boxes A, B, C or D to show the correct
answer.

14 Trevor MacDonald

    A works in the British Clothing Industry.

    B models ties.

    C writes for a Caribbean magazine.

    D reads the news on television.

A
B
C
D

15 Choosing a tie is easy for Trevor because

    A he has lots of suits.

    B he has lots of shirts.

    C he wears only plain ties.

    D he wears only plain suits.

A
B
C
D

16 On cold grey days, Trevor usually

    A takes no notice of the weather.

    B feels depressed all day.

    C wears a grey tie.

    D wears a colourful tie.

A
B
C
D

[20]

17 Which word best sums up Trevor's personality?

A	
B	
C	
D	

A   conventional

B   outrageous

C   diverse

D   adventurous

THIRD PART

Listen to this interview with Angela Blackstone, author of books for children.
For questions 18–24 tick a box to show whether the statements are true or false according
to what Angela says.

According to Angela Blackstone:

	True	False
18 informative books are inevitably dull.		
19 the main function of children's books is to give information.		
20 books are the best medium for showing how other people think.		
21 children are genuinely interested in fantasy books.		
22 illustrations can confuse children.		
23 it is better to illustrate your own books.		
24 children are more critical of her books than adults.		

PAPER 5 INTERVIEW (15–20 minutes)

You will be asked to take part in a conversation with a group of other students or with your teacher. The conversation will be based on one particular topic area or theme, for example holidays, work, food.

Of course each interview will be different for each student or group of students, but a *typical* interview is described below.

* At the start of the interview you will be asked to talk about one of the photographs among the Interview Exercises at the back of the book.

* You will then be asked to discuss one of the passages at the back of the book. Your teacher may ask you to talk about its content, where you think it comes from, who the author or speaker is, whether you agree or disagree with it, and so on. You will *not* be asked to read the passage aloud, but you may quote parts of it to make your point.

* You may then be asked to discuss for example an advertisement, a leaflet, extract from a newspaper etc. Your teacher will tell you which of the Interview Exercises to look at.

* You may also be asked to take part in an activity with a group of other students or your teacher. Your teacher will tell you which section among the Interview Exercises you should look at.

Practice Test 2

PAPER 1 READING COMPREHENSION (1 hour)

Answer all questions. Indicate your choice of answer in every case **on the separate answer sheet** *already given out, which should show your name and examination index number. Follow carefully the instructions about how to record your answers. Give* **one answer only** *to each question. Marks will not be deducted for wrong answers: your total score on this test will be the number of correct answers you give.*

SECTION A

In this section you must choose the word or phrase which best completes each sentence. **On your answer sheet** *indicate the letter A, B, C, or D against the number of each item 1 to 25 for the word or phrase you choose.*

1   After listening to all the arguments I am now of the .... that there should be no new road.
   A attitude   B opinion   C thought   D idea

2   He didn't know anyone at the wedding .... than the bride and groom.
   A except   B other   C apart   D rather

3   Protests died down when they realised that the new tax .... to only 50p a week.
   A added   B reached   C approached   D amounted

4   It was a serious quarrel, and they took a long time to make it ....
   A over   B away   C out   D up

5   As he approached the end of the race he found it hard to .... his speed.
   A carry on   B keep on   C maintain   D persevere

6   The accused was given a short sentence as he had committed only a .... offence.
   A subordinate   B minimal   C secondary   D minor

7   If he discovers the truth, there's no telling what .... happen.
   A should   B shall   C would   D might

8 New legislation makes it possible for the Government to ....
   protest marches.
   A ban   B forestall   C inhibit   D deny

9 She .... wanted a house overlooking the sea.
   A particularly   B strongly   C essentially   D extremely

10 'Most people .... the Government's economic policy as a
    success,' claimed the spokesman.
    A measure   B consider   C look on   D believe

11 For centuries Rome was the .... power in the Mediterranean.
    A utmost   B superlative   C overruling   D supreme

12 She caught a .... of the thief as he made his get-away.
    A glance   B sight   C glimpse   D flash

13 Edinburgh is known .... the Athens of the North.
    A for   B by   C as   D with

14 At the universities of Oxford and Cambridge the .... of teachers
    to students is very high.
    A proportion   B number   C ratio   D percentage

15 The little boy was continually .... the ornaments.
    A tripping up   B falling down   C breaking up   D knocking over

16 We can judge the success of your scheme only by taking ....
    account the financial benefits over the next few years.
    A into   B out   C from   D over

17 I couldn't tell what time it was because workmen had removed the
    .... of the clock.
    A hands   B pointers   C arms   D fingers

18 For my birthday, I was given a writing set .... two pens,
    envelopes and notepaper.
    A involving   B comprising   C consisting   D holding

19 I wrote to my bank manager .... to getting a loan.
    A in the hope   B on the question   C with the aim   D with a view

20 Those men were appointed by the directors and are .... only to
    them.
    A accountable   B dependable   C privileged   D controlled

21 The boy's mother was .... in by his lies.
    A drawn   B taken   C pulled   D caught

22 Children who are praised for their work are always .... on to do better.
    A encouraged   B approved   C inspired   D spurred

23 After many years as a doctor, he had become .... to scenes of human distress.
    A hardened   B experienced   C expert   D unemotional

24 The wheels .... as the car went over an icy patch.
    A skipped   B slid   C skidded   D slipped

25 Members of the aristocracy don't .... a great deal of power nowadays.
    A practise   B wield   C sway   D manage

SECTION B

In this section you will find after each of the passages a number of questions or unfinished statements about the passage, each with four suggested answers or ways of finishing. You must choose the one which you think fits best according to the passage. **On your answer sheet ,** *indicate the letter A, B, C or D against the number of each item 26–40 for the answer you choose. Give* **one answer only** *to each question. Read each passage right through before choosing your answers.*

FIRST PASSAGE

The Bay filled the middle distance, stretching out of sight on both sides, and one's eye naturally travelled in a great sight-seeing arc: skimming along the busy Shoreline Freeway, swerving out across the Bay via the long Esseph Bridge to the city's dramatic skyline, dark downtown skyscrapers posed against white residential hills, from which it leapt across the graceful curves   5
of the Silver Span suspension bridge, gateway to the Pacific, to alight on the green slopes of Miranda County.
    This vast panorama was agitated, even early in the morning, by every known form of transportation – ships, yachts, cars, trucks, trains, planes, helicopters and hovercraft – all in simultaneous motion, reminding Philip of   10
the brightly illustrated cover of a children's book. It was indeed, he thought, a perfect marriage of Nature and Civilisation, this view, where one might take in at a glance the consummation of man's technological skill and the finest splendours of the natural world. The harmony he perceived in the scene was, he knew, illusory. Just out of sight to his left a cloud of smoke   15

hung over the great military and industrial port of Ashland, and to his right the oil refineries of St Gabriel fumed into the limpid air. The Bay, which winked so prettily in the morning sun, was, people said, poisoned by industrial waste and untreated effluent.

For all that, Philip thought, almost guiltily, framed by his living-room 20 window and seen at this distance, the view still looked very good indeed.

Morris Zapp was less entranced with his view – a vista of dank back gardens, rotting sheds and dripping laundry, huge ill-looking trees, grimy roofs, factory chimneys and church spires – but he had discarded this criterion at a very early stage of looking for accommodation in an English 25 industrial town. You were lucky, he had quickly discovered, if you could find a place that could be kept at a temperature appropriate to human organ-isms, equipped with the more rudimentary amenities of civilised life, and decorated in a combination of colours and patterns that didn't make you want to vomit on sight. He had taken an apartment on the top floor of a 30 huge old house owned by an Irish doctor and his extensive family. Dr O'Shea had converted the attic with his own hands for the use of an aged mother, and it was to the recent death of this relative, the doctor impressed upon him, that Morris owed the good fortune of finding such enviable accommodation vacant. Morris didn't see this as a selling point himself, but 35 O'Shea seemed to think that the apartment's sentimental associations were worth at least an extra five dollars a week to an American torn from the bosom of his own family.

26 What sort of movement is suggested by the verbs used to describe the eye's progress in the first paragraph?
   A smooth
   B rapid
   C interrupted
   D reluctant

27 Why did Philip look 'almost guiltily' (line 20) at the view?
   A He realised its beauty was deceptive.
   B He felt responsible for the pollution.
   C He felt he was wasting time looking at it.
   D He knew he had a better view than most people.

28 Which factor did Morris consider most important when choosing accommodation?
   A a tolerable view
   B a pleasant landlord
   C a reasonable rent
   D an efficient heating system

29 Dr O'Shea expected Morris to find the history of the apartment
   A   amusing.
   B   comforting.
   C   depressing.
   D   exciting.

30 What is Morris's attitude towards accommodation in England?
   A   He is charmed by the quaintness of the houses.
   B   He finds the contrast with America interesting.
   C   He is prepared to make the best of it.
   D   He wishes he had stayed at home.

31 Which of these statements, comparing the views from the two windows, is correct?
   A   Philip's view is more peaceful.
   B   Philip's view is more homely.
   C   Morris's view is more restricted.
   D   Morris's view is more uplifting.

SECOND PASSAGE

During the nineteenth century the tranquil surface of English village life often hid a surprising depth of personal bitterness and organised class conflict. In the 1830s the countryside was literally set alight in the outbreak of arson and machine-breaking that accompanied the 'Labourers' Revolt'. In the 1870s the 'Revolt of the Field' led by Joseph Arch attempted to establish   5
a farm workers' union, but was met with organised hostility and petty vindictiveness from farmers and landowners. After a time rural peace was restored and Arch's union was broken, but the everyday tensions of class conflict lay only slightly beneath the surface.

  As with any isolated and largely self-contained community the agricul-   10
tural village was often the object of a fierce loyalty among its inhabitants. From its customs and traditions the village could draw upon a strong sense of identity and morality which, looking back, may easily be mourned in a more impersonal, amoral and uncertain modern world. This sense of certainty was probably the village's greatest source of strength. Inevitably the   15
boundaries of what was and was not considered permissible in village life were much clearer in the nineteenth century, as they were in Victorian society generally. This conferred a sense of order on village life, a sense of place both geographical and social. For those villagers who accepted their 'place' this state of affairs created a not altogether unwelcome sense of   20
security. For those who found the social order unacceptable – the rebellious, the ambitious or simply the single-minded – the village could become a prison, dispiriting and mean-spirited, restricting the individualist by the vicious purveyance of gossip and innuendo.

32 Why did Arch's union fail?
    A   because of personal feelings
    B   because he committed crimes
    C   because it was not well-organised
    D   because the employers opposed it

33 How did the majority of villagers regard their village?
    A   They regretted any changes.
    B   They were proud to live independent of the cities.
    C   They were very committed to it.
    D   They found its strict morality repressive.

34 According to the passage, compared with nineteenth-century villagers, people in modern society are
    A   less hypocritical.
    B   less secure.
    C   better educated.
    D   more law-abiding.

35 Which aspect of village life troubled people who did not accept their 'place'? (line 20)
    A   the immorality of the landowners
    B   the subservience of the inhabitants
    C   the cruel punishments
    D   the narrowness of outlook

THIRD PASSAGE

All at once Hazel was coming in through the french windows, pulling off gardening gloves, and Bill was entering through the door, both at once. So I only had time to take one quick look at her before I turned to face him. All very confusing. What that first glimpse showed me was that time had thickened her figure but didn't seem to have made much difference to her face. It still had good skin and youthful outlines. She was holding a bunch of roses – must have been cutting them in the garden while waiting for me. The gardening gloves lent a delightfully informal touch. It was quite an entrance, though Bill spoilt it a bit by making his at the same time.

Bill seemed longer and thinner. His tightly massed hair had a tinge of grey. Apart from that, twenty years had done nothing to him, except deepen the lines of thoughtfulness that had already, when I knew him, begun to spread across his face. Or was that all? I looked at him again, more carefully, as he looked away from me at Hazel. Weren't his eyes different somehow? More inward-looking than ever? Gazing in not merely at his thoughts, but at something else, something he was keeping hidden or perhaps protecting.

Then we were chattering and taking glasses in our hands, and I came back to earth. For the first ten minutes we were all so defensive, so carefully probing, that nobody learnt anything. Bill had forgotten me altogether, that much was clear. He was engaged in getting to know me from scratch, very cautiously so as not to hit a wrong note, with the object of getting me to contribute a big subscription to his African project. I kept trying to absorb details about Hazel, but Bill was talking earnestly about African education, and the strain of appearing to concentrate while actually thinking about his wife proved so great that I decided it would be easier just to concentrate. So I did. I let him hammer away for about ten more minutes, and then the daughter, who seemed to be acting as parlour-maid, showed in another visitor. Evidently we were to be four at lunch.

36 What effect had time had on Hazel and Bill?
   A They had both lost weight.
   B They were more withdrawn.
   C They hadn't changed at all.
   D They had changed in subtle ways.

37 When they all started talking, the writer
   A relaxed at last.
   B stopped dreaming.
   C spoke most to Hazel.
   D began to remember things.

38 The writer found the first part of their conversation
   A sentimental.
   B irritating.
   C uninformative.
   D trivial.

39 Why did Bill speak seriously?
   A He wanted some money from the writer.
   B He did not remember the writer.
   C His wife was present.
   D He was talking about the past.

40 In the end the writer found Bill's conversation
   A monotonous.
   B convincing.
   C thought-provoking.
   D instructive.

PAPER 2   COMPOSITION   (2 hours)

*Write **two only** of the following composition exercises. Your answers must follow exactly the instructions given. Write in pen, not pencil. You are allowed to make alterations, but see that your work is clear and easy to read.*

1   Describe the toys you most enjoyed playing with as a child. (About 350 words)

2   What are the qualities and qualifications needed by an expert salesman? (About 350 words)

3   Write a story which begins or ends with the words, 'So he was not dead after all'. (About 350 words)

4   'Elderly tourist knocked down by motorist at dangerous crossing.'
Write **two** on-the-spot statements made to the police using 100–150 words for each,
 (i) by the pedestrian,
(ii) by the local motorist.

5   Basing your answer on your reading of the prescribed text concerned, answer *one* of the following. (About 350 words)

PATRICIA HIGHSMITH: *The Talented Mr Ripley*
'He had to be lively as well as talented not to get caught.' Discuss.

JOHN OSBORNE: *The Entertainer*
Describe the ways in which the other members of the Rice family struggle to cope with their feelings of failure and loss.

D. H. LAWRENCE: *Selected Tales*
What do we learn about life in a mining community at the time Lawrence was writing?

PAPER 3 USE OF ENGLISH (2 hours)

SECTION A

1 *Fill each of the numbered blanks in the following passage with* **one** *suitable word.*

One question that is often asked is whether people can be induced to commit criminal acts under hypnosis. .... (1) fairly recently scholars tended to think .... (2); they argued that an order instructing a person to act in ways which were very much .... (3) to his moral and ethical ideas would not be .... (4) out.

However, a number of experiments have recently .... (5) conducted that show this conclusion is not universally true. In one .... (6) experiment the experimenter demonstrated the power of nitric acid .... (7) the subject by throwing a penny .... (8) it. The penny, of .... (9), was completely destroyed and the subject was .... (10) to realise the tremendous destructive power of nitric acid. .... (11) the subject's view of the bowl of acid was .... (12) by the experimenter, an assistant substituted .... (13) it a like-sized bowl of harmless methylene-blue water, ... (14) continuously boiling by the presence in it of minuscule droplets of barium peroxide. The hypnotised subject .... (15) then ordered to throw the dish .... (16) the assistant, who was present in the same room. .... (17) these conditions it was .... (18) to induce various subjects to throw .... (19) they considered to be an .... (20) dangerous acid into the face of a human being.

[31]

2 *Finish each of the following sentences in such a way that it means exactly the same as the sentence printed before it.*

> EXAMPLE: Immediately after his arrival things went wrong.
>
> ANSWER: No sooner *had he arrived than things went wrong.*

a) Many people were severely critical of the proposals for the new motorway.

There was ....

b) For a teacher of her experience and ability, discipline was not a problem.

For such ....

c) There was no precedent for the King's resignation.

Never ....

d) The police were informed of the identity of the murdered man.

The identity ....

e) The fate of the two climbers is unknown.

It is a mystery ....

f) He was suspended for two matches for swearing at the referee.

Swearing at the referee earned ....

g) Although he was not guilty they executed him.

In spite of ....

h) People who haven't been abroad shouldn't criticise foreign customs.

Nobody who ....

3 *Fill each of the blanks with a suitable word or phrase.*

> EXAMPLE: Even if I had stood on a chair, *I wouldn't have been able to* reach the light bulb.

a) That cheese is mouldy; .... I were you.

b) As long as it leads to a good career .... to me what course of study you follow.

[32]

c) You had a lucky escape. You .... killed.

d) You'll have to .... of that old dustbin.
There's a hole in it.

e) In order to get better results .... adding
a little more flour.

f) 'You should go and look for a job, not sit around doing nothing.'

'Why don't you mind ....?'

4 *For each of the sentences below, write a new sentence* **as similar as possible in
meaning to the original sentence,** *but using the word given. This word* **must not
be altered in any way.**

> EXAMPLE: Not many people attended the meeting.
> **turnout**

> ANSWER: *There was a poor turnout for the meeting.*

a) The girl's behaviour was incomprehensible to the Head Teacher.
loss

....

b) They will think your nephew stole the money.
suspected

....

c) Fred tried hard to start the car, but without success.
matter

....

d) The Arnolds consider Henry a good friend.
look

....

e) Everyone but Jane failed to produce the correct answer.
succeeded

....

[33]

f) The new ambassador is well-informed about current affairs.
   wide

   ....

g) They were brought up in a conventional, middle-class way.
   theirs

   ....

h) That United will beat City is a foregone conclusion.
   bound

   ....

SECTION B

5 *Read the following passage, then answer the questions which follow it.*

In nature, fighting is such an ever-present process that its behaviour mechanisms and weapons are highly developed. Almost every animal capable of self-defence from the smallest upwards fights furiously when it is cornered and has no means of escape.

However, in another respect the fight between hunter and hunted is   5
not a fight in the real sense of the word: the stroke of the paw with which a lion kills his prey may resemble the movements that he makes when he strikes his rival but the inner motives of the hunter are basically different from those of the fighter. The buffalo which the lion fells provokes his aggression as little as the appetizing turkey which I have just seen hang-   10
ing in the larder provokes mine. The difference in these inner drives can clearly be seen in the expression movements of the animal: a dog about to catch a hunted rabbit has the same kind of excited happy expression as he has when he greets his master or awaits some longed-for treat. Growling, laying the ears back, and other well-known expression move-   15
ments of fighting behaviour occur when predatory animals are afraid of a wildly resisting prey, and even then the expressions are only suggested.

The opposite process, the counter-offensive, of the prey against the predator, is more nearly related to genuine aggression. Social animals in particular take every possible chance to attack the eating enemy that   20
threatens their safety. This process is called 'mobbing'. The survival value of this attack on the hunter is self-evident. Even if the attacker is small and defenceless, he may do his enemy considerable harm. For example, if a sparrowhawk is pursued by a flock of warning wagtails, his hunting is spoiled for the time being. And many birds will mob an owl if   25

they find one in the day-time, and drive it so far away that it will hunt somewhere else the next night.

In some social animals such as jackdaws and many kinds of geese, the function of mobbing is particularly interesting. In jackdaws, its most important survival value is to teach the young inexperienced birds what 30 a dangerous eating-enemy looks like, which they do not know instinctively. For just such educational reasons, geese and ducks may gather together in intense excitement to learn that a fox – anything furry, red-brown, long-shaped and slinking – is extremely dangerous.

Besides this didactic function, mobbing of predators by jackdaws 35 and geese still has the basic, original one of making the enemy's life a burden. Jackdaws actively attack their enemy, and geese apparently intimidate it with their cries, their thronging and their fearless advance. The great Canada Geese will even follow a fox overland in a close phalanx, and I have never known a fox in this situation try to catch one 40 of his tormentors. With ears laid back and a disgusted expression on his face, he glances back over his shoulder at the trumpeting flock and trots slowly – so as not to lose face – away from them.

Among the larger, more defence minded grazing animals which en masse are a match for even the biggest predators, mobbing is particularly 45 effective; according to reliable reports, zebras will molest even a leopard if they catch him on a plain where cover is sparse. Moreover, the reaction of social attack against the wolf is so ingrained in domestic cattle and pigs that one can sometimes land oneself in danger. Once, when I was out with my dog, I was obliged to jump into a lake and swim for safety 50 when a herd of young cattle half encircled us and advanced threateningly; and when he was in Southern Hungary during the First World War my brother spent a pleasant afternoon up a tree with his Scotch terrier under his arm, because a herd of half-wild Hungarian swine, disturbed while grazing in the wood, encircled him. 55

a) In what circumstances will small animals fight? ....

    ....

b) What is the 'real sense' of 'fight' as suggested by the writer (line 6)?

    ....

c) Explain clearly how the lion feels when he is attacking his prey.

    ....

    ....

⋙►

[35]

d) Explain in your own words the circumstances in which hunting animals display signs of aggression.

....

....

....

e) Explain what is meant by 'counter-offensive' in line 18. ....

....

f) What precisely is meant by the word 'mobbing' as used in line 21? ....

....

g) In what ways can 'mobbing' be particularly effective? ....

....

h) What is the 'didactic function' referred to in line 35? ....

....

i) What word in the fourth paragraph could replace the word 'didactic' (line 35)?

....

j) Explain in your own words the phrase 'making the enemy's life a burden' (lines 36–37).

....

....

k) In what ways are the tactics used by jackdaws against their enemies different from those used by geese?

....

....

....

l) Explain in your own words why the fox moves away *slowly* (line 43). ....

....

m) In what circumstances are some grazing animals a match for even the biggest predators?

....

....

n) What reason does the writer give to explain why cattle and pigs will attack a pet dog?

....

....

o) What evidence is there in the passage to suggest that domestic cattle and pigs are dangerous to humans?

....

....

....

p) In a paragraph of 80–100 words, summarise what the writer says about the ways different animals 'mob' their enemies, and indicate the different reasons they have for this 'mobbing'.

....

....

....

....

....

....

....

....

[37]

....

....

....

....

....

....

....

PAPER 4 LISTENING COMPREHENSION
(about 30 minutes)

FIRST PART

You will hear a talk about Fats Domino, the jazz musician.
For questions 1–8 fill in the missing information by writing brief answers.

FATS DOMINO

At what age did he make his first record? ① ....

How often did he meet Louis Armstrong? ② ....

When did he record the song 'Blueberry Hill'? ③ ....

Did Fats Domino write it? ④ ....

Is he still recording now? ⑤ ....

How many children has he?

boys? ⑥ ....   girls? ⑦ ....

How many of his children play the piano? ⑧ ....

SECOND PART

You will hear a discussion about dinosaurs.
For each of the questions 9–18 tick (✓) one box to show whether the statement is true or false.

	True	False
9 A 100 million-year-old dinosaur skeleton has been discovered.		
10 The new species of dinosaur was a flesh eater.		
11 This is one of the most exciting discoveries of the century.		
12 The important discovery was made by a well-known scientist.		
13 The fossilised remains were found in a forest.		
14 The fossil hunter walked onto a dinosaur claw.		
15 The fossil hunter damaged the claw.		
16 The rare fossils were kept in a cupboard.		
17 The fossil collector was willing to give away the dinosaur bones.		
18 The dinosaur has already been named after its discoverer.		

THIRD PART

*You will hear a recorded telephone announcement giving details for visitors to
Edinburgh, in Scotland.*
For questions 19–28 fill in the missing information in the spaces provided.

19 Bus numbers ...., ..., ... and .... go to the zoo.

20 The dance band starts playing at .... in Princess Street Gardens.

21 Duddingston Kirk was built in ....

22 Lothian Regional Transport's telephone number is ....

23 Tours of the countryside around Edinburgh leave from ....

24 Wellhouse Tower is at the top of the Royal Mile near ....

25 The Camera Obscura was placed in the Tower in ....

26 The shop at the tower sells ...., ... and

....

27 At the .... in Leven Street you can hear Scottish
Traditional singing in the evening.

28 The Tourist Information Centre telephone number is ....

PAPER 5   INTERVIEW   (15–20 minutes)

You will be asked to take part in a conversation with a group of other students or with your teacher. The conversation will be based on one particular topic area or theme, for example holidays, work, food.

Of course each interview will be different for each student or group of students, but a *typical* interview is described below.

* At the start of the interview you will be asked to talk about one of the photographs among the Interview Exercises at the back of the book.

* You will then be asked to discuss one of the passages at the back of the book. Your teacher may ask you to talk about its content, where you think it comes from, who the author or speaker is, whether you agree or disagree with it, and so on. You will *not* be asked to read the passage aloud, but you may quote parts of it to make your point.

* You may then be asked to discuss for example an advertisement, a leaflet, extract from a newspaper etc. Your teacher will tell you which of the Interview Exercises to look at.

* You may also be asked to take part in an activity with a group of other students or your teacher. Your teacher will tell you which section among the Interview Exercises you should look at.

Practice Test 3

PAPER 1   READING COMPREHENSION   (1 hour)

Answer all questions. Indicate your choice of answer in every case **on the separate answer sheet** *already given out, which should show your name and examination index number. Follow carefully the instructions about how to record your answers. Give* **one answer only** *to each question. Marks will not be deducted for wrong answers: your total score on this test will be the number of correct answers you give.*

SECTION A

In this section you must choose the word or phrase which best completes each sentence. **On your answer sheet** *indicate the letter A, B, C, or D against the number of each item 1 to 25 for the word or phrase you choose.*

1   One condition of this job is that you must be .... to work at weekends.
    A available   B capable   C acceptable   D accessible

2   A relief .... has been set up to help earthquake victims.
    A fund   B donation   C treasury   D collection

3   The prison was so well guarded that any thought of escape was
    ....
    A despairing   B aimless   C desperate   D pointless

4   Supposing I .... to agree to your request, how do you think the other students would feel?
    A would   B am   C were   D could

5   I hope you won't take .... if I tell you the truth.
    A annoyance   B offence   C resentment   D irritation

6   His failure .... great disappointment to his parents.
    A forced   B made   C caused   D provided

7   The government's new safety pamphlet .... against smoking in bed.
    A declares   B advises   C emphasises   D maintains

⟫▶

8   When he had finished the apple he threw the .... into the bin.
    A heart   B pith   C core   D kernel

9   Two months is .... time to allow for the job to be completed.
    A profuse   B protracted   C ample   D extensive

10 Don't jump .... conclusions; we don't yet know all the relevant
    facts.
    A into   B up   C to   D for

11 Even at that early stage the school felt that she .... a good chance
    of passing her exams.
    A stood   B gained   C possessed   D took

12 No-one appreciated his work during his lifetime, but .... it is clear
    that he was a great artist.
    A in the aftermath   B by the time   C in retrospect   D in this
    eventuality

13 Although they had suffered heavy losses, the commanders refused to
    .... defeat.
    A grant   B assent   C concede   D acquiesce

14 The government spends vast sums on defence while public services are
    being cut ....
    A up   B back   C through   D over

15 Even .... for inflation he thought it was a good investment.
    A considering   B taking account   C allowing   D calculating

16 He looked like an Englishman, but his foreign accent gave him ....
    A in   B away   C up   D over

17 Even the most .... drivers feel an urge to break the speed-limit
    occasionally.
    A lawful   B legitimate   C law-abiding   D judicial

18 While politicians argue about nuclear weapons, ordinary people are simply
    concerned .... staying alive.
    A of   B with   C for   D in

19 I turned down his offer to stay as I did not wish to .... upon his family.
    A interfere   B disturb   C invade   D impose

20 There was a storm .... I had never experienced before.
    A such as   B as which   C with which   D for such

21 As soon as the consumer protection law was passed, some manufacturers
    began to .... to have it changed.
    A object   B revolt   C campaign   D protest

22 I'm so tired that I can't take .... what you're saying.
    A up   B out   C in   D on

23 The first time he spoke in public he was .... with nerves.
    A overcome   B inhibited   C numbed   D frozen

24 In order to give up smoking, you need to exercise great ....
    A abstinence   B obstinacy   C endeavour   D will-power

25 For people with hearing difficulties, telephones with volume controls
    provide the best ....
    A solution   B response   C reply   D result

SECTION B

*In this section you will find after each of the passages a number of questions or unfinished
statements about the passage, each with four suggested answers or ways of finishing. You
must choose the one which you think fits best according to the passage.* **On your answer
sheet** , *indicate the letter A, B, C or D against the number of each item 26–40 for the
answer you choose. Give* **one answer only** *to each question. Read each passage right
through before choosing your answers.*

FIRST PASSAGE

The intention of *The List of Books* is to furnish an 'imaginary library' of some
three thousand volumes in which a reasonably literate person can hope to
find both instruction and inspiration, art and amusement. It was the French
writer André Malraux who first coined the term to describe the choice of the
world's art which a man might make to furnish his own private museum.   5
Modern printing, Malraux proceeded to argue, has actually made such a
collection a practical possibility. Masterpieces which men of the eighteenth
century and before had to travel to see are now within the reach of all who
can afford a postcard or a newspaper supplement. Mechanical reproduction
has removed art from the hands of the few and made it accessible to all.   10
Printing has done the same for books: the paperback is scarcely more expen-
sive than the fine art print.
    Our problem is no longer one of access; it is more likely to be one of
choice. How are we to choose among the thousands of available titles? To
enter a library is immediately to be seized by a kind of panic; one risks starv-   15
ing among such plenty. The confession that one does not know what to read

next, or where to begin in an unfamiliar subject, is shameful in a society in
which nobody wishes to be a beginner and where naivety is likely to earn
the scorn accorded to all newcomers. This book seeks to be a kind of reader's
ticket to that immense library which man has put together ever since he first   20
began to leave a written record of his experiences and his opinions.

Our first notion as compilers of this book was to supply lists of unadorned titles in each of the standard library categories. But to give no
information about the books proposed would be to leave the reader in the
bemused condition of a guest at a crowded party to whom the host has noth-   25
ing more to say than 'You know everybody here, of course'. So we decided
that it was essential to give a brief account of each recommended book,
however laughable or superficial an authority on the subject might find it.

It is no scandal not to find your favourite book in these pages; we are
not judging, though we have been obliged to choose. This is, in short,   30
an imaginary library, not *the* imaginary library. It can, and should be,
supplemented by further reading and broader research. In fact, the collation
of these lists has been enough to pull down our vanity; for the more one
looks at what is available in an unfamiliar field, the more urgent the desire
one feels to abandon the affectations of the editor and assume the modesty   35
of the student.

26   The *List of Books* is
     A   an index of early printed books.
     B   a complete catalogue of English books.
     C   a personal selection of books.
     D   a collection of rare books.

27   Nowadays the great works of art are more
     A   protected.
     B   familiar.
     C   scattered.
     D   valuable.

28   The vast number of books available means that people
     A   find their demands easily satisfied.
     B   spend a lot of time reading.
     C   are uncertain what to read.
     D   are scornful of new subjects.

29   Readers would find a list of 'unadorned titles' (lines 22–23)
     A   reassuring.
     B   unhelpful.
     C   stimulating.
     D   absurd.

30 When they had completed their list, the authors
    A   felt proud of their knowledge.
    B   wanted to give up reading.
    C   were aware of their own ignorance.
    D   felt dissatisfied with the results.

SECOND PASSAGE

By three o'clock in the afternoon there was nothing left for Hilliard to do. He had been to the Army and Navy Stores and gone slowly from counter to counter buying what he needed, and after that, looking, looking. The war had brought out a fever like that of Christmas among manufacturers and salesmen, there were so many possible things to buy, expressly for the soldiers in France. Hilliard watched people buying them, mothers, aunts, sisters, wives, who had no idea what might be really suitable, who wanted to send something extra, who were misled by the advertisements and the counter staff into ordering useless gifts to be packed up and sent. He saw bullet-proof waistcoats and fingered them in amazement, remembering the bullets, saw leather gauntlets, too stiff and thick and hot, saw ornamental swords and pistols of use only to gamekeepers, saw the shining new metal of entrenching tools and spurs.

But he wanted to buy something then, something that was entirely superfluous, an extravagance, a gift to himself. He moved about among the women and could see nothing, felt as he had felt on a day's outing from school, when the money his father had given him burned a hole in his pocket and he was almost in tears at the frustration of finding nothing he desired to buy.

He spent more than two pounds on a pale cane walking-stick with a round silver knob, and, carrying it out into the sunlit street, felt both foolish and conspicuous, as though he had succumbed to the temptation of some appalling vice. The cane looked so new. At school it had been the worst possible taste to have an unblemished leather trunk with bright buckles: the thing had been to kick it, or to drop it several times from the luggage van on to the station platform. Now, he felt like a soldier who had not yet been to France, because of the cane: people looked at him and he wanted to shout at them, 'I have been before, I have been and now I am going back. *I know.*'

31 The advice given by counter staff was
    A   well-informed.
    B   hurried.
    C   unreliable.
    D   unclear.

32 The gifts for soldiers at war were
    A   impractical.
    B   expensive.
    C   festive.
    D   in short supply.

33   What did Hilliard hope to buy as a gift for himself?
    A   something he really needed
    B   something suitable for war
    C   something to remind him of his father
    D   something he would enjoy

34   How did the attempt to buy something affect Hilliard?
    A   It made him cry.
    B   It reminded him of his childhood.
    C   It made him feel proud.
    D   It pleased him.

35   Hilliard found the cane embarrassing because
    A   he had had one like it at school.
    B   it was not worth the money.
    C   it made him look inexperienced.
    D   he couldn't take it to France.

THIRD PASSAGE

A.   The lane was very, very old. The hedges were so high that in summer they would form a tunnel of green. Earthworks stood at the summit of the hill above the cottage. Here the people of earlier times had lived and died, worked their magic and honoured their dead, until later invaders had arrived, and driven them out, and lived off a past that was none of their own.

B.   Much of what is now empty was not always so bare. The mountains were covered in trees at one time, but climatic change and the felling of timber for smelting iron means that there are no trees there now. The many ruined farms, and the stone walls which are built over the hills in all except the bleakest places, remind us that this is not quite untreated nature.

C.   The mountains are older than anything else in the world. No water has ever covered them, and the sun, who has watched them for countless ages, may still discern in their outlines forms that were his before our globe was torn from his bosom. They are sinking beneath the newer lands. Their main mass is untouched, but at the edge their outposts have been cut off and stand knee-deep, throat-deep, in the advancing soil. They are like nothing else in the world, and a glimpse of them makes the breath catch.

D.   There is a level surface of limestone. This is quite bare and divided into curly-edged but squarish blocks, called clints, separated by deep ditches known as dykes. This is the result of rainwater dissolving the stone along regular lines of weakness in its structure.

36 In which passage does the writer describe the landscape through human imagery?
    A.   B.   C.   D.

37 Which passage implies that change took place through human conflict?
    A.   B.   C.   D.

38 How many of these passages describe social change?
    A   all of them
    B   two of them
    C   three of them
    D   none of them

39 What do we learn from passage C?
    A   Farmers are reclaiming the land around the mountains.
    B   The weight of the mountains is causing them to sink.
    C   The level of the land near the mountains is changing.
    D   The heat of the sun is drying up the land.

40 Which passage makes the greatest emotional impact?
    A.   B.   C.   D.

PAPER 2   COMPOSITION   (2 hours)

*Write **two only** of the following composition exercises. Your answers must follow exactly the instructions given. Write in pen, not pencil. You are allowed to make alterations, but see that your work is clear and easy to read.*

1   Write a descriptive account of a holiday which ended in disaster. (About 350 words)

2   Describe what you think could be done to reduce the amount of violence in modern life. (About 300 words)

3   Write about your own astrological birth sign. Is this a true indication of your personality? (About 300 words)

4   Explain the object and the rules of any game you enjoy playing, and give some hints on how to win. (About 300 words)

5   Basing your answer on your reading of the text concerned, answer **one** of the following. (About 350 words)

JOHN OSBORNE: *The Entertainer*
Is *The Entertainer* basically a funny or a sad play?

D. H. LAWRENCE: *Selected Tales*
In most of the stories in this selection the people tend to be unhappy. Choose **three** of the stories and explain why the main characters are unhappy.

PATRICIA HIGHSMITH: *The Talented Mr Ripley*
'Of all the characters in the novel the reader feels most sorry for Marge.' How far is this true?

PAPER 3 USE OF ENGLISH (2 hours)

SECTION A

1 *Fill each of the numbered blanks in the following passage with* **one** *suitable word.*

We all know that wood burns and that brick and concrete do not.
.... (1) would seem to be an excellent reason for .... (2)
sure that timber .... (3) forms part of the structure of modern
houses, but in fact about a quarter of all new houses in Britain
.... (4) built around timber frames with an outer lining of bricks.
.... (5) theory, the building regulations laid .... (6) by
the government ensure that these houses are safe from .... (7), but
the safety provisions themselves could .... (8) introducing a new
hazard which has .... (9) to do with the .... (10) that
wood burns.

The regulations demand that the structure of a timber-framed house
should be .... (11) well protected that it .... (12) remain
standing .... (13) after fire has swept .... (14) from
bottom to top. But the non-flammable materials that protect the timber can
heat .... (15) very quickly and radiate heat back .... (16)
the room, feeding the fire and .... (17) it to burn more rapidly. The
regulations .... (18) this hazard and up to .... (19) very
little research has been .... (20) to solve the problem.

2 *Finish each of the following sentences in such a way that it means exactly the same as the sentence printed before it.*

> EXAMPLE: Immediately after his arrival things went wrong.
>
> ANSWER: No sooner *had he arrived than things went wrong.*

a) The only way to eliminate world terrorism is by united opposition.

Only by ....

....

b) If she hadn't insisted on kissing everyone goodbye she would have caught the train.

If it hadn't ....

....

c) The fisherman's life was one of great poverty.

Throughout ....

d) Someone has suggested abolishing income tax.

It ....

e) I do not enjoy cooking for five hungry children.

Cooking ....

f) My parents find fault with everything I do.

No matter ....

g) I certainly don't intend to reply to that rude letter from Edward.

I have ....

h) Simon had not expected that he would feel so weak after the operation.

The operation left ....

3 *Fill each of the blanks with a suitable word or phrase.*

> EXAMPLE: Even if I had stood on a chair, *I wouldn't have been able to* reach the light bulb.

a) In spite .... unwell the Prime Minister continued her tour of the factory.

b) Helen's away this week, so it's .... ring her.

c) Should you ever be .... of assistance, contact this number.

d) I am .... painted pink to match the carpet and curtains.

e) Frescobaldi's theory about perpetual motion was fascinating, but it was

impossible .... practice.

f) The party was great: you really .... come.

4   *For each of the sentences below, write a new sentence* **as similar as possible in meaning to the original sentence,** *but using the word given. This word* **must not be altered** *in any way.*

EXAMPLE: Teaching doesn't really suit her.
           cut

ANSWER: *She isn't really cut out for teaching.*

a) The rate of inflation has fallen steadily during recent months.
   decline

   ....

b) It was Derek who pointed the mistake out to me.
   attention

   ....

c) They were on the point of cancelling the match when the opposition arrived.
   call

   ....

d) Not many people attended the concert.
   poorly

   ....

e) The train is five minutes late in leaving.
due

....

f) This licence is valid until December 31st 1987.
expiry

....

g) One essay is just as bad as the other.
choose

....

h) Most doctors agree that smoking is bad for your health.
harm

....

SECTION B

5 *Read the following passage, then answer the questions which follow it.*

Many critics of our British 'Public Schools' consider that far more stress
is placed upon achievements in athletics than in the academic sphere,
and, in particular, complain against games being compulsory. We are
told that it is tyranny to compel boys with no athletic bent to spend
hours of misery on a cricket or football field, when, if left to themselves,   5
they would occupy their time far more usefully and enjoyably in some
profitable hobby. The drawback to this argument lies in the facile
assumption that every non-athlete has some profitable hobby. This is not
true; and even if it were, model engineering or stamp-collecting is no
substitute for being out in the fresh air, exercising the muscles and   10
having contact with other human beings.

Yet the youthful idolising of athletes, which tends to upset a boy's
sense of values and may do actual harm to the objects of this hero-
worship, is a very different matter. The schoolboy athlete may suffer
enormously through being adorned at an early age with a spurious halo   15
of artificial light. From Preparatory School to University his career is a
triumphal procession. Then he becomes a legend for the future, one of
the greatest products of the school that is proud to call him her son,
although she may have taught him nothing except to play football –
which he could do already. Not until he hangs up his football boots for   20
the last time and takes his stock out into the open market of the world

does he realise his true value – or the lack of it. It would be better for everybody if this tinsel pageantry were stripped from games at an early stage. The boy who is good at games is entitled to the admiration of his fellows; they will certainly never put the scholar on the pedestal which the athlete now occupies, but the community must lay emphasis on the essential triviality of talents that are merely physical, unless we are willing that our ideals should be those of the jungle.

But there are still those devotees of sport who support the emphasis laid on school games for much deeper reasons, and for whom sport is a kind of religion. To them the sporting spirit is the finest attitude with which to face life, since its possessor is very conscious of his obligations to the community. Yet the truth about the religion of sport is that it does not deliver the goods; it fails to produce sportsmen. In actual fact, games have practically no effect on character, for a selfish man will play his games selfishly in spite of all that has been talked about the team spirit, while a chivalrous man will be chivalrous in his games. Games afford an opportunity for showing the spirit within; they are a vehicle for virtue or for vice; and it is for this that we should value them, not as some miraculous process for making a bad man good or a crooked man straight. If we support the system of compulsory games, let it be for the right reasons.

a) What is meant by 'boys with no athletic bent' (line 4)? ....

....

b) Why is the assumption in line 7 described as 'facile'? ....

....

c) Who are 'the objects of this hero-worship' (lines 13–14)? ....

....

d) What is the 'spurious halo of artificial light' referred to in lines 15–16? ....

....

e) What does the word 'stock' (line 21) mean as used in the passage? ....

....

f) What is the attitude of schoolboys to intellectual ability? ....

.... ⫸►

g) What are referred to as 'those of the jungle' (line 28)? ....

....

....

h) In what way can sport be regarded as a 'religion' (line 31)? ....

....

i) What is it that 'does not deliver the goods' (lines 33–34)? ....

....

j) What is meant by 'sportsmen' in line 34? ....

....

k) Give another phrase for 'a vehicle for virtue or for vice' (lines 38–39). ....

....

l) What reasons are suggested in the passage against attaching too much importance to sport? With which of these does the writer agree? (60–80 words)

....

....

....

....

....

....

....

....

....

....

....

....

PAPER 4 LISTENING COMPREHENSION
(about 30 minutes)

FIRST PART

You will hear a telephone conversation in which Frances Drew asks Mr Harding about an Arts Club. For questions 1 to 10, fill in the missing information on Frances Drew's note-pad. Some information has already been filled in for you.

Arts Club Secretary - Tel. 363

Calendar - collect from library on ① ....

Membership fee ~ £2.50 per adult

Social events:
     club evenings take place ② ....

     at the Beach Pavilion, ③ ....

Choir practices held on ④ ....

To join the choir contact the ⑤ ....

Membership fee to be sent to ⑥ ....

Cheque payable to ⑦ ....

Members receive ⑧ ....

Activities sections:
     Acting group ⑨ "The .... "
     Musical activities ~ choir and ⑩ ....
     ....
     Literary and discussion groups etc.

SECOND PART

You will hear part of a radio programme in which aids to help handicapped children are discussed. For each of the questions 11–19 tick (✓) one box to show whether the statement is true or false.

	True	False
11 Pafupi had to buy some parts for his tricycle.		
12 Pafupi used very simple tools.		
13 Pafupi made his tricycle without any help from others.		
14 Pafupi was the first person to make a polio tricycle.		
15 Pafupi made his tricycle narrow to help it go round corners.		
16 Pafupi's tricycle could go backwards.		
17 They made a copy of Pafupi's tricycle in case the original was lost.		
18 Pafupi liked both Kennet Westmacott's new ideas.		
19 You can get details of how to make a Pafupi tricycle directly from the B.B.C.		

THIRD PART

You will hear a man and a woman discussing their holiday plans.
For questions 20–24 tick (✓) one of the boxes A, B, C or D.

20   Why is the woman doubtful about the holiday?

   A   They need £500 extra.

   B   They need a new car.

   C   They are short of money.

   D   They haven't got time.

A	
B	
C	
D	

21   The man is irritated because his wife

   A   doesn't want to go on holiday.

   B   wants to be in England for Christmas.

   C   doesn't think holidays are necessary.

   D   thinks family holidays are best.

A	
B	
C	
D	

22   The woman suggests taking a

   A   shorter holiday.

   B   holiday in Europe.

   C   winter holiday.

   D   holiday at home.

A	
B	
C	
D	

23   Why is the woman against asking her mother for money?

   A   She would rather ask the bank manager.

   B   She knows they can't repay her mother.

   C   She feels they should be able to manage alone.

   D   She thinks her mother would refuse.

A	
B	
C	
D	

24 How does the man's attitude change during the conversation?

    A from anger to resignation

    B from optimism to frustration

    C from disappointment to acceptance

    D from irritation to alarm

A	
B	
C	
D	

FOURTH PART

You will hear someone asking Lily about her job as a translator.
For questions 25–29 tick (✓) one of the boxes A, B, C or D.

25 What offer of translation work is Lily still considering?

    A a series of travel books

    B a book about Greece

    C an Italian translation

    D a book about four different countries

A	
B	
C	
D	

26 Why is she worried about working with other translators?

    A They might not understand each other easily.

    B She might not get on well with the others.

    C They might translate words differently.

    D She might not be able to work as fast as the others.

A	
B	
C	
D	

27 Why is she unsure about the latest job she's been offered?

    A Because she doesn't want to work on her own.

    B Because she isn't interested in the subject matter.

    C Because it would be too hard.

    D Because she wouldn't be paid as well as usual.

A	
B	
C	
D	

28 Why did she start to work as a translator?

A   She wanted to help a friend.

B   She was advised to by her teacher.

C   She was offered a job.

D   She met a translator in a pub.

A	
B	
C	
D	

29 In what respect was Lily suited to start work as a translator?

A   She lived abroad after getting her degree.

B   She had passed an exam after two years.

C   She had worked for a French company in Germany.

D   She was an Associate Member of the Translator's Guild.

A	
B	
C	
D	

PAPER 5 INTERVIEW (15–20 minutes)

You will be asked to take part in a conversation with a group of other students or with your teacher. The conversation will be based on one particular topic area or theme, for example holidays, work, food.

Of course each interview will be different for each student or group of students, but a *typical* interview is described below.

* At the start of the interview you will be asked to talk about one of the photographs among the Interview Exercises at the back of the book.

* You will then be asked to discuss one of the passages at the back of the book. Your teacher may ask you to talk about its content, where you think it comes from, who the author or speaker is, whether you agree or disagree with it, and so on. You will *not* be asked to read the passage aloud, but you may quote parts of it to make your point.

* You may then be asked to discuss for example an advertisement, a leaflet, extract from a newspaper etc. Your teacher will tell you which of the Interview Exercises to look at.

* You may also be asked to take part in an activity with a group of other students or your teacher. Your teacher will tell you which section among the Interview Exercises you should look at.

Practice Test 4

PAPER 1   READING COMPREHENSION   (1 hour)

Answer all questions. Indicate your choice of answer in every case **on the separate answer sheet** *already given out, which should show your name and examination index number. Follow carefully the instructions about how to record your answers. Give* **one answer only** *to each question. Marks will not be deducted for wrong answers: your total score on this test will be the number of correct answers you give.*

SECTION A

In this section you must choose the word or phrase which best completes each sentence. **On your answer sheet** *indicate the letter A, B, C, or D against the number of each item 1 to 25 for the word or phrase you choose.*

1   It was too late to .... of the contract.
    A back out   B back down   C back up   D back away

2   By going in person to the office which .... the forms she was able to get what she wanted.
    A controlled   B offered   C disseminated   D issued

3   The student failed to meet the necessary .... for admission to the course.
    A fulfilments   B requirements   C qualities   D aptitudes

4   .... of recent political developments he was taken by surprise on his arrival in the capital.
    A Unexpected   B Unacquainted   C Unaware   D Unknowing

5   She always .... the smell of fresh bread with her mother, who loved baking.
    A remembered   B associated   C exemplified   D attributed

6   After the theft of his car he put in an insurance .... for £3,000.
    A account   B invoice   C assessment   D claim

7   He'll be very upset if you .... his offer of help.
    A turn away   B turn from   C turn down   D turn against

»»→

8 Prizes are awarded .... the number of points scored.
   A resulting from   B adding up   C presented to   D according to

9 The committee took just thirty minutes to .... the conclusion that action was necessary.
   A judge   B make   C decide   D reach

10 She bought the mansion .... that she would make a fortune out of her new novel.
    A speculating   B considering   C assuming   D estimating

11 After his girlfriend left him, George determined never .... in love again.
    A to fall   B falling   C for to fall   D having fallen

12 The job applicant told her interviewer that she would jump .... the chance to work for such a prestigious firm.
    A to   B for   C on   D at

13 The ability to .... work is the sign of a good manager.
    A discharge   B appoint   C deputise   D delegate

14 He failed to .... the authorities of his change of address.
    A certify   B report   C notify   D acquaint

15 The children .... at the ease with which the circus acrobats performed their routine.
    A amazed   B marvelled   C surprised   D baffled

16 When her millionaire father died, the heiress .... a fortune.
    A came into   B came at   C came through   D came to

17 When he examined the gun the detective's suspicion turned into ....
    A certainty   B confirmation   C reality   D conclusion

18 The seat belt can be altered to .... for differences in the size of the passenger.
    A permit   B adjust   C calculate   D allow

19 Because of rapid technological progress, the computers being made today will be .... in five years' time.
    A outdone   B extinct   C obsolete   D retired

20 Few pleasures can equal .... of a cool drink on a hot day.
    A it   B that   C such   D this

21 I'll just .... an eye over these figures before you type them.
    A cast   B fling   C toss   D throw

22 His emotional problems .... from the attitudes he encountered as
    a child, I think.
    A stem   B flourish   C root   D sprout

23 This book is full of practical .... on home decorating and repairs.
    A helps   B tips   C aids   D clues

24 If we bend the rules for one person it will .... a dangerous
    precedent.
    A create   B cause   C invent   D make

25 The little boy was left in .... his grandmother during his parents'
    absence.
    A charge   B care of   C care   D the charge of

SECTION B

In this section you will find after each of the passages a number of questions or unfinished statements about the passage, each with four suggested answers or ways of finishing. You must choose the one which you think fits best according to the passage. **On your answer sheet,** *indicate the letter A, B, C or D against the number of each item 26–40 for the answer you choose. Give* **one answer only** *to each question. Read each passage right through before choosing your answers.*

FIRST PASSAGE

The forest from which Man takes his timber is the tallest and most impressive plant community on Earth. In terms of Man's brief life it appears permanent and unchanging, save for the seasonal growth and fall of the leaves,
but to the forester it represents the climax of a long succession of events.

No wooded landscape we see today has been forest for all time. Plants   5
have minimum requirements of temperature and moisture and, in ages past,
virtually every part of Earth's surface has at some time been either too dry or
too cold for plants to survive. However, as soon as climatic conditions
change in favour of plant life, a fascinating sequence of changes occurs,
called a primary succession.   10
First to colonize the barren land are the lowly lichens, surviving on bare
rock. Slowly, the acids produced by these organisms crack the rock surface,
plant debris accumulates, and mosses establish a shallow root-hold. Ferns
may follow and, with short grasses and shrubs, gradually form a covering of
plant life. Roots probe even deeper into the developing soil and eventually   15

large shrubs give way to the first trees. These grow rapidly, cutting off sunlight from the smaller plants, and soon establish complete domination – closing their ranks and forming a climax community which may endure for thousands of years.

Yet even this community is not everlasting. Fire may destroy it outright   20
and settlers may cut it down to gain land for pasture or cultivation. If the land is then abandoned, a secondary succession will take over, developing much faster on the more hospitable soil. Shrubs and trees are among the early invaders, their seeds carried by the wind, by birds and lodged in the   25
coats of mammals.

For as long as it stands and thrives, the forest is a vast machine storing energy and the many elements essential for life.

26 Why does the forest strike mankind as permanent?
    A   The trees are so tall.
    B   It is renewed each season.
    C   Our lives are short in comparison.
    D   It is an essential part of our lives.

27 What has sometimes caused plants to die out in the past?
    A   interference from foresters
    B   variations in climate
    C   the absence of wooded land
    D   the introduction of new types of plants

28 In a 'primary succession' (line 10), what makes it possible for mosses to take root?
    A   the type of rock
    B   the amount of sunlight
    C   the amount of moisture
    D   the effect of lichens

29 What conditions are needed for shrubs to become established?
    A   Ferns must take root.
    B   The ground must be covered with grass.
    C   More soil must accumulate.
    D   Smaller plants must die out.

30 Why is a 'secondary succession' (line 22) quicker?
    A   The ground is more suitable.
    B   There is more space for new plants.
    C   Birds and animals bring new seeds.
    D   It is supported by the forest.

SECOND PASSAGE

Some of Winifred Holtby's friends wanted to see this biography published soon after her death in order to catch a supposed topical market and to forestall the appearance of half-informed studies. For those who loved her, I fully realise how painful and exasperating it has been to wait for a complete account of her life, based upon adequate knowledge and that growth of understanding which only years of close friendship can bring. My apologies are due to them for the many explanations offered of the simple fact that I did not write this book earlier because I did not want to. I knew that, if I wrote quickly, I should very soon repent of what I had written.

It would have been easy enough, on the strength of memory and a superficial glance through a mass of papers which Winifred left me, to construct a readable record of her life within a few months of her death. Anyone accustomed to writing books could produce such a volume; and she had not been a week in her grave before a number of publishers – though not my own – had invited me to do so. From the standpoint of sales such a course would doubtless have benefited my interests as well as theirs, but I cannot believe that it would have assisted Winifred's reputation.

A hasty portrait may be good journalism, but almost without exception it is bad biography. The chief essential of biography is truth, and truth is seldom served by hurried studies however topical and efficient. In practice, such work usually proves to be short-lived to precisely the degree that it is topical.

The closer one person has been to another, the greater the need for time to elapse in order that the bitterness of loss and the arbitrary selections of memory may be modified by perspective and detachment, by the thorough investigation of available material, and most of all by the quiet process of unhurried reflection. Even within the past few months, many facts of Winifred's life and character have become clear to me.

I can therefore only plead for understanding and forgiveness when I say that I could not have produced a truthful study of the best friend whom life has given me in the months directly following her death.

31 There was an urgent demand for a biography of Winifred Holtby from
    A   journalists who required information about the subject.
    B   readers who wanted to know more about Holtby's past.
    C   publishers who wanted to make money.
    D   scholars interested in Holtby's literary standing.

32 The author delayed writing the biography because of
    A   her close involvement with the subject.
    B   the suddenness of Holtby's death.
    C   confusion over so much information.
    D   pressure of work.

33   At the time of Holtby's death, the author was a(n)
    A   inexperienced writer.
    B   established writer.
    C   popular writer.
    D   wealthy writer.

34   Compared with journalistic writing, good biography is
    A   less up-to-date.
    B   more efficiently written.
    C   less concerned with accuracy.
    D   less likely to be forgotten.

35   Before writing the biography, the author wanted to
    A   form new opinions.
    B   find a new publisher.
    C   spend time in contemplation.
    D   be forgiven by her friends.

THIRD PASSAGE

Cardiologists divide us into two types, according to how our personality affects our heart. Type A individuals are highly competitive, innately hostile, fast eating and rapid talking, whilst B types drown in the milk of human kindness and are sublimely indifferent to the passage of time. It is an uncomfortable fact that A's die twice as frequently from heart disease as B's,   5
even when the risks of cigarettes, alcohol and cream buns are taken into account.

Personality is to a large extent genetically endowed – A-type parents usually beget A-type offspring. But the environment must also have a profound effect, since if competition is important to the parents, it is likely to   10
become a major factor in the lives of their children.

One place where children soak up A traits is school, which is, by its very nature, a highly competitive institution. Too many schools adopt the 'win at all costs' ethic and measure their success by sporting achievements. The current mania for making children compete against their peers or against the   15
clock produces a two-tier system, in which competitive A types seem in some way better than their B type fellows. Addiction to winning can have dangerous consequences: remember that Pheidippides, the first marathon runner, dropped dead seconds after croaking: 'Rejoice, we conquer!'

By far the worst form of competition in schools is the disproportionate   20
emphasis on examinations. It is a rare school that allows pupils to concentrate on those things they do well. The merits of competition by examination are dubious enough, but competition in the certain knowledge of failure is positively harmful.

Obviously, it is neither practical nor desirable that all A youngsters   25
change into B's. The world needs both types, and schools have an important
duty to try to fit a child's personality to his possible future employment. It is
a fallacy, for instance, that people successful in business are full of competitive zeal; there are many B types in top management.

If the preoccupation of schools with academic work was lessened, more   30
time might be spent teaching children surer values. Perhaps selection for the
caring professions, especially medicine, could be made less by good grades
in chemistry and more by such considerations as sensitivity, altruism and
compassion. It is surely a mistake to choose our doctors exclusively from A
type stock. B's are important and should be encouraged.   35

36   According to cardiologists Type A individuals are usually
    A   greedy.
    B   affectionate.
    C   aggressive.
    D   carefree.

37   Children develop into Type A rather than Type B individuals because of
    A   parental attitudes.
    B   pressure from their friends.
    C   differences in social class.
    D   hereditary defects.

38   What feature of schools does the author criticise?
    A   Intelligent students become discouraged.
    B   There is a limited choice of subjects.
    C   Some individuals are undervalued.
    D   Sport is rated below academic achievement.

39   What is particularly harmful about examinations?
    A   Failure rates are high.
    B   The wrong students succeed.
    C   Unsuitable subjects are set.
    D   Some students are bound to fail.

40   Entrants to the medical profession at present are selected on the basis of
    their
    A   academic achievements.
    B   personal qualities.
    C   competitive spirit.
    D   interest in society.

PAPER 2 COMPOSITION (2 hours)

*Write **two only** of the following composition exercises. Your answers must follow exactly the instructions given. Write in pen, not pencil. You are allowed to make alterations, but see that your work is clear and easy to read.*

1   Describe in about 350 words, **either** (i) a doctor's waiting room
                                         or   (ii) a visit to the dentist.

2   'Education is not only for the young.' Discuss. (About 300 words)

3   Write a story entitled 'An Unwelcome Visitor'. (About 350 words)

4

O.T.T. St. James Crescent London W. 1.

The best for :Low fares

safety

service

comfort

in-flight entertainments

When you travel in style–It's got to be –O.T.T.

After seeing this advertisement you decided to fly O.T.T. However, you were extremely disappointed by the flight. Write a letter to the Company explaining that the advertisement was seriously misleading. (About 250 words)

5   Basing your answer on your reading of the text concerned, answer **one** of the following. (About 350 words)

JOHN OSBORNE: *The Entertainer*
Do you feel that *The Entertainer* takes up any social issues seriously, or is it simply entertainment?

[70]

D. H. LAWRENCE: *Selected Tales*
Illustrate from the stories how Lawrence's attitude to his characters is often a mixture of ridicule and compassion.

PATRICIA HIGHSMITH: *The Talented Mr Ripley*
'Tom is a violent and pitiless killer yet the reader wants him to escape and not be arrested.' How far is this true?

PAPER 3 USE OF ENGLISH (2 hours)

SECTION A

1 *Fill each of the numbered blanks in the following passage with* **one** *suitable word.*

My first holiday in France suddenly made me realise how a child must feel
trying to make himself understood without an .... (1) command of
language. When I went shopping I used to rehearse my various set
.... (2) for each market stall, and, choosing .... (3) that
were not busy, I .... (4) edge near, trying to .... (5)
someone's eye. The words never came .... (6) as I intended, but
nods, smiles, pointing and a .... (7) isolated words (with no
refinements .... (8) as verbs correctly conjugated) served the
.... (9) well, and I felt wonderfully triumphant.

The stallholders were friendly and unfailingly helpful .... (10)
seeing that I got .... (11) I wanted and .... (12)
I understood the financial part of the transaction. They also
.... (13) me .... (14) encouragement to learn new words
and phrases and I even began to .... (15) about the weather, the
sea and the sand. And .... (16) one of them began to correct
.... (17) grammar, but I was too young and sensitive and was
.... (18) into confusion. I reverted to .... (19) anxious
and afraid of trying in .... (20) I was wrong.

2 *Finish each of the following sentences in such a way that it means exactly the same as the sentence printed before it.*

EXAMPLE: Immediately after his arrival things went wrong.

ANSWER: No sooner *had he arrived than things went wrong.*

a) Thanks to his aunt's legacy of £10,000 he was able to buy the house he wanted.

Had his ....

b) They were unable to finish their game of tennis because of a heavy shower.

A heavy shower ....

c) I didn't realise he was your brother until I saw the photograph.

It was only ....

d) I haven't been to see them for over a year.

It's ....

e) The President is the statesman I admire most of all.

There is ....

f) Don't you wish you could get out more in the evenings?

Don't you get fed ....

g) 'It certainly wasn't me who took your car!' said Bob.

Bob denied ....

h) It's nobody's fault that the meeting was cancelled.

Nobody ....

3 *Fill each of the blanks with a suitable word or phrase.*

EXAMPLE: Even if I had stood on a chair, *I wouldn't have been able to* reach the light bulb.

a) The man was .... to ten years in prison.

b) She'll never learn to play the piano, ...
hours she practises.

⋙►

[73]

c) You'd better .... socks up or you'll fail
    the exam.

d) They all turned up at the meeting, with ....
    the treasurer, who was ill.

e) It's hard at first when you become widowed, but people eventually ....
    .... alone.

f) This is one ....
    I have ever read.

4   *For each of the sentences below, write a new sentence* **as similar** *as possible in*
    meaning to the original sentence, *but using the word given. This word* **must not**
    be altered in any way.

    EXAMPLE: Not many people attended the meeting.
             turnout

    ANSWER: *There was a poor turnout for the meeting.*

a) There is less chance that Olsen will become champion after his recent defea
    blow

    ....

b) It's a waste of time to try and explain anything to Tony.
    worth

    ....

c) Most people consider that stealing is wrong.
    everybody

    ....

d) Give in to him and you'll regret it.
    stand

    ....

e) Final year students don't have to attend lectures.
    optional

    ....

f) Please would you send me further details of the job advertised?
    grateful

    ....

g) The critic had a low opinion of the new play.
    much

    ....

h) I doubt if Mary will want to see Christopher in the circumstances.
    hardly

    ....

SECTION B

5   *Read the following passage, then answer the questions which follow it.*

In 1920 my father realized it was time to return to civilian life, and he
managed to become the representative of the German press agency in
Amsterdam. From here he took some leave almost before he had begun
his work, and set off in the direction of the Soviet Union in order to trace
the whereabouts of his parents and his sister. Since it was difficult to   5
travel in Russia at a time when so many people were bent on getting out
of it, he managed to integrate himself into a large group of prisoners-of-
war being repatriated. They knew about the Revolution, of course, and
they also knew that it was they who were the starvelings so recently
awakened from their slumbers; their enthusiasm overflowed into song   10
and simple rapture as the day of their return to the paradise of the
workers approached. Many of them had bicycles which they had ac-
quired at the end of their captivity, and these undreamed-of vehicles
became the status symbols of the new dawn, grasped possessively by
those about to cross the threshold of Utopia. As soon as the ship   15
steamed into Narva harbour, at the frontier between the Soviet Union
and Estonia, the bicycles were confiscated for the urgent needs of the
war against the Poles, and the returned prisoners, including my father,
were locked into cattle trucks to be shunted to recruiting centres further
in the hinterland for induction into the Red Army.   20
    As the train crept through the night with its embittered complement
of silent men, cringing amid the dung and straw, my father planned his
escape. Stops were frequent, and, at one of them, he forced open the
door. The first traces of dawn were visible, flecks in the icy sky, and, in
the distance, the unseen evidence of a city, a glint, a certain unmistak-   25
able heaviness about the horizon, the roar of silence, as in a shell. He

dropped off the train with his suitcase, full of chocolate, rashers of bacon
and lumps of sugar, all precious items in troubled times. An hour or two
later, he was in the heart of Leningrad. He spoke very little Russian,
which did not seem much of a hindrance when the Herculean nature of   30
his labour is taken into consideration, which was quite simply to find an
old man and his wife and daughter in a country which covers one-sixth
of the earth's surface. He began by meeting my mother, and that seemed
to be a step in the right direction. At least I think so.

a)   What was the author's father before he became the representative of the
     German press agency?

     ....

b)   Explain in your own words the phrase 'to trace the whereabouts' (lines
     4–5).

     ....

     ....

c)   What is the meaning of 'bent on' (line 6)? ....

     ....

d)   What was the advantage of joining a group of prisoners-of-war? ....

     ....

e)   What did the prisoners expect to find on their return to Russia? ....

     ....

f)   Why are bicycles described as 'undreamed-of' in line 13? ....

     ....

g)   What is 'the threshold of Utopia' referred to in line 15? ....

     ....

h)   Why were the men 'embittered' (line 21)? ....

     ....

i) What does the phrase 'dung and straw' (line 22) tell us about the men's transport?

....

j) Why are the contents of the suitcase described as 'precious items in troubled times' (line 28)?

....

k) What impressions does the author give about his father's search for his relations?

....

....

l) Summarise, in a paragraph of 50–70 words, what we learn from the passage about the Soviet Union at this time.

....

....

....

....

....

....

....

....

....

....

....

PAPER 4 LISTENING COMPREHENSION
(about 30 minutes)

FIRST PART

Listen to Mr and Mrs Muddle talking about their children and grandchildren and answer questions 1–15 below. If the information is not given, write 'not given' as the answer. One question has been done for you.

Son

How many children does he have?	(1)	boy(s)
	(2)	girl(s)
How far away does he live from his parents?	(3)	
How often does he see his parents?	(4)	
What is his job?	(5)	

1st daughter

How many children does she have?	(6)	boy(s)
	(7)	girl(s)
How far away does she live from her parents?	(8) **12 miles**	
How often does she see her parents?	(9)	
What is her job?	(10)	

2nd daughter Jennifer

How many children does she have?	(11)	boy(s)

(12) .... girl(s)

How far away does she live from her parents? (13) ....

How often does she see her parents? (14) ....

What is her job? (15) ....

SECOND PART

You will hear an interview with a man who has written a book about computers. For questions 16–21 tick (✓) one of the boxes A, B, C or D to show the best answer.

16 Computer manufacturers want to build computers that

   A   think more accurately than people.

   B   think faster than people.

   C   reveal the way people think.

   D   seem to think like people.

A	
B	
C	
D	

17 How does the human brain differ from the computer?

   A   It is interpretive.

   B   It is logical.

   C   Its parts are inter-linked.

   D   Its parts are rigidly separated.

A	
B	
C	
D	

18 Compared with a person's brain, the CRAY-1 has

   A   less capacity.

   B   more thinking power.

   C   a better memory ability.

   D   a pigeon-sized brain.

A	
B	
C	
D	

≫≫►

19 Adrian Berry thinks that computers will become

    A   our inferiors.

    B   our masters.

    C   our superiors.

    D   our successors.

A	
B	
C	
D	

20 Computers can cause trouble in the home because

    A   mothers could neglect their children.

    B   children could neglect their school-work.

    C   husbands could neglect their wives.

    D   wives could neglect their husbands.

A	
B	
C	
D	

21 The author's overall attitude towards computers is

    A   enthusiastic.

    B   ambivalent.

    C   dismissive.

    D   suspicious.

A	
B	
C	
D	

THIRD PART

You will hear an interview with a man who used to be a farmer. For questions 22–25 tick (✓) one of the boxes A, B, C or D to show the best answer.

22 Why has the speaker retired from farming?

    A   His brother ended the partnership.

    B   His nephew bought him out.

    C   The farm had grown too big.

    D   The farm needed too much money.

A	
B	
C	
D	

23 The changes which the speaker made

   A   involved buying heavy equipment.

   B   became outdated.

   C   involved levelling the land.

   D   were unnecessary.

A	
B	
C	
D	

24 What does his new job offer the speaker?

   A   more money

   B   greater opportunities

   C   new training

   D   shorter hours

A	
B	
C	
D	

25 According to the speaker, farming

   A   requires a long term outlook.

   B   offers financial security.

   C   is very satisfying for young people.

   D   is more profitable on a small scale.

A	
B	
C	
D	

FOURTH PART

You will hear an announcement about facilities available in a Science Museum. For each of the questions 26–28 tick (✓) one of the boxes A, B, C or D to show the correct answer.

26 Which of the following items can be bought at the stall for £1.50?

A

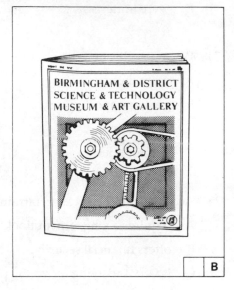

B

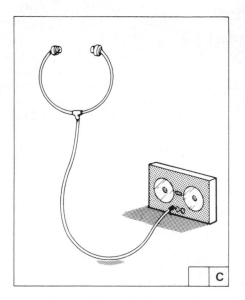

C

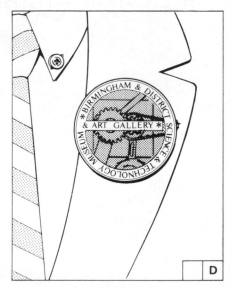

D

27   What is a museograph?

A

B

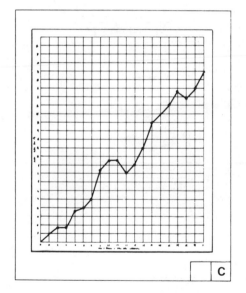

C

D

28 Which advertisement is correct?

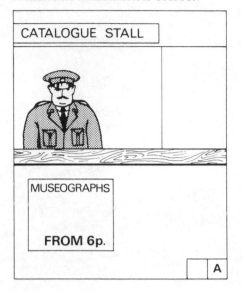

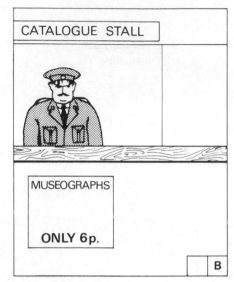

PAPER 5 INTERVIEW (15–20 minutes)

You will be asked to take part in a conversation with a group of other students or with your teacher. The conversation will be based on one particular topic area or theme, for example holidays, work, food.

Of course each interview will be different for each student or group of students, but a *typical* interview is described below.

* At the start of the interview you will be asked to talk about one of the photographs among the Interview Exercises at the back of the book.

* You will then be asked to discuss one of the passages at the back of the book. Your teacher may ask you to talk about its content, where you think it comes from, who the author or speaker is, whether you agree or disagree with it, and so on. You will *not* be asked to read the passage aloud, but you may quote parts of it to make your point.

* You may then be asked to discuss for example an advertisement, a leaflet, extract from a newspaper etc. Your teacher will tell you which of the Interview Exercises to look at.

* You may also be asked to take part in an activity with a group of other students or your teacher. Your teacher will tell you which section among the Interview Exercises you should look at.

Practice Test 5

PAPER 1   READING COMPREHENSION   (1 hour)

Answer all questions. Indicate your choice of answer in every case **on the separate answer sheet** *already given out, which should show your name and examination index number. Follow carefully the instructions about how to record your answers. Give* **one answer only** *to each question. Marks will not be deducted for wrong answers: your total score on this test will be the number of correct answers you give.*

SECTION A

In this section you must choose the word or phrase which best completes each sentence. **On your answer sheet** *indicate the letter A, B, C, or D against the number of each item 1 to 25 for the word or phrase you choose.*

1   All his companies had been successful and he was known to be
.... rich.
A absolutely   B completely   C extremely   D thoroughly

2   On .... to power the new President announced a programme of social reforms.
A arriving   B reaching   C achieving   D coming

3   No one really knows who composed this piece of music, but it has been
.... to Bach.
A identified   B associated   C referred   D attributed

4   .... had the van turned the corner than the wheel came off.
A Scarcely   B No longer   C Hardly   D No sooner

5   The judge said the thief had shown complete .... for the law.
A ignorance   B disregard   C disobedience   D negligence

6   The Director's personality was undoubtedly a .... in the company's success.
A feature   B factor   C characteristic   D cause

7   My .... on life has changed a lot since leaving university.
A outlook   B view   C approach   D purpose

[86]

8   Although the coach had not thought her a good tennis player at first, she
    .... to be a champion.
    A came round   B came out   C turned up   D turned out

9   The bad weather meant .... the rocket launch for 48 hours.
    A delaying   B to delay   C having delayed   D was delayed

10 She went to a lot of .... and expense to choose and send that present.
    A anxiety   B trouble   C difficulty   D care

11 .... her inexperience her failure to secure the contract was not
    surprising.
    A In view of   B By virtue of   C With regard to   D In recognition of

12 This machine is .... to overheat if you leave it switched on.
    A susceptible   B probable   C conducive   D liable

13 It is a brave man who .... for his beliefs when under attack.
    A stands out   B stands forward   C stands up   D stands by

14 I wonder if there's any connexion .... his disappearance and the theft?
    A to   B between   C about   D of

15 This company is in the .... of modern technological research.
    A foreground   B foretaste   C forefront   D foremost

16 It is difficult to say exactly what .... the present dissatisfaction
    with the management.
    A brought in   B brought about   C brought out   D brought over

17 From the top of the hill the village looks quite close, but distances are
    ....
    A deceptive   B surprising   C false   D illusory

18 Apparently one person .... ten now attends a university in this country.
    A of   B over   C in   D from

19 The noise of the machinery .... the words of the factory manager.
    A covered   B suppressed   C drowned   D deadened

20 The drivers have rejected proposals to end the strike and the other workers
    have come out in ....
    A consent   B return   C sympathy   D collaboration

21 He was always finding .... with his daughter's friends.
    A blame   B lack   C mistake   D fault

⟫▶

22 After her eye operation she had to wear an eye .... for protection.
    A patch   B veil   C glass   D screen

23 Her refusal to join us is nothing .... of ridiculous.
    A less   B more   C short   D far

24 The professor's .... theory is that singing preceded speech.
    A preferable   B pet   C fond   D fancied

25 A local charity benefited from the .... of the annual summer fête.
    A earnings   B income   C pay   D proceeds

SECTION B

In this section you will find after each of the passages a number of questions or unfinished statements about the passage, each with four suggested answers or ways of finishing. You must choose the one which you think fits best according to the passage. **On your answer sheet ,** *indicate the letter A, B, C or D against the number of each item 26–40 for the answer you choose. Give* **one answer only** *to each question. Read each passage right through before choosing your answers.*

FIRST PASSAGE

The decline of traditional religion in the West has not removed the need for men and women to find a deeper meaning behind existence. Why is the world the way it is and how do we, as conscious individuals, fit into the great scheme?

There is a growing feeling that science, especially what is known as the new physics, can provide answers where religion remains vague and faltering. Many people in search of a meaning to their lives are finding enlightenment in the revolutionary developments at the frontiers of science. Much to the bewilderment of professional scientists, quasi-religious cults are being formed around such unlikely topics as quantum physics, space-time relativity, black holes and the big bang.

How can physics, with its reputation for cold precision and objective materialism, provide such fertile soil for the mystical? The truth is that the spirit of scientific enquiry has undergone a remarkable transformation over the past 50 years. The twin revolutions of the theory of relativity, with its space-warps and time-warps, and the quantum theory, which reveals the shadowy and unsubstantial nature of atoms, have demolished the classical image of a clockwork universe slavishly unfolding along a predetermined pathway. Replacing this sterile mechanism is a world full of shifting indeterminism and subtle interactions which have no counterpart in daily experience.

To study the new physics is to embark on a journey of wonderment and paradox, to glimpse the universe in a novel perspective, in which subject and object, mind and matter, force and field, become intertwined. Even the creation of the universe itself has fallen within the province of scientific enquiry.

The new cosmology provides, for the first time, a consistent picture of how all physical structures, including space and time, came to exist out of nothing. We are moving towards an understanding in which matter, force, order and creation are unified into a single descriptive theme.

Many of us who work in fundamental physics are deeply impressed by the harmony and order which pervades the physical world. To me the laws of the universe, from quarks to quasars, dovetail together so felicitously that the impression there is something behind it all seems overwhelming. The laws of physics are so remarkably clever they can surely only be a manifestation of genius.

26 The author says people nowadays find that traditional religion is
   A   a form of reassurance.
   B   inadequate to their needs.
   C   responding to scientific progress.
   D   developing in strange ways.

27 Scientists find the new cults bewildering because they are
   A   too reactionary.
   B   based on false evidence.
   C   derived from inappropriate sources.
   D   too subjective.

28 Which phrase in paragraph 3 suggests that the universe is like a machine?
   A   cold precision and objective materialism
   B   the shadowy and unsubstantial nature of atoms
   C   slavishly unfolding along a predetermined pathway
   D   shifting indeterminism and subtle interactions.

29 The new physics is exciting because it
   A   offers a comprehensive explanation of the universe.
   B   proves the existence of a ruling intelligence.
   C   incorporates the work of men of genius.
   D   makes scientific theorising easier to understand.

30 The author of this passage is
   A   a minister of religion.
   B   a research scientist.
   C   a science fiction writer.
   D   a journalist.

SECOND PASSAGE

Simpkins' period of office as a local politician was nearly over. He felt reluctant to go through all the bother of standing for re-election. His tentative voicing of this feeling shocked Baden.

'You're never going to give up after all this time?'

'That's the point about it, Baden. Perhaps I've gone on too long. I feel tired, somehow.'

'Tired! Look at me. I'm not tired and I can give you ten years. How long have you been on the council now?'

'Eighteen years.'

Baden snorted. It was nothing beside his thirty-five years of unbroken service, during which he'd been three times mayor. Simpkins winked at Baden's wife, Maude, and she, looking up from her embroidery, gave him back a small smile. Simpkins sometimes felt that it was not a mere ten years which separated Baden and himself, but two world wars. The years of his boyhood before the first war were the golden age that Baden looked back to. 'It all ended after that,' he had said more than once. 'We never saw its like again.' It was no use arguing that the quality of life was better for more people now, because Baden wouldn't have it. 'There were men working for my father who had six, seven and eight children. They brought them up all right though they hadn't much money. Now it's all grab. They want money, cars, drink and holidays abroad. And nobody's happy.'

'Were they ever?' Simpkins wondered. 'Was an obsession with keeping body and soul together a necessary condition of human happiness?'

They were talking in the new bungalow Baden had built where Maude could find amusement watching the traffic go by.

'A drink, anyway, Tom?'

'I'd not say no to a drop of whisky, Baden.'

The floorboards trembled as Baden crossed the room.

'How much do you weigh?' Simpkins asked.

'Too much,' Maude chipped in.

'Oh, I don't know,' Baden said sharply. 'Fifteen and a half stone.'

'Add a bit to that,' Simpkins thought.

'You must have iron legs. I'm bigger than you and I don't weigh that much.'

'You don't have my belly, though, Tom.' Baden placed his two hands on the swell of his waistcoat. 'It's good solid stuff, not just a bag of wind.'

Maude tut-tutted – 'Really, Baden' – while Simpkins laughed.

'There's nothing the matter with me – in spite of Maude always going on about it.'

'It's no use me saying anything,' Maude said. 'He stopped listening to me years ago.'

Simpkins sensed some bitterness behind the mild comment. Always headstrong, and domineering where he met resistance, Baden instinctively treated women as people to be kept in their place.

31 For how long have Simpkins and Baden been politicians together?
    A   for an equal length of time
    B   since the First World War
    C   for ten years
    D   for the last eighteen years

32 When the two men discuss the past
    A   they are inclined to lose their tempers.
    B   Simpkins claims that life used to be harder.
    C   Baden thinks that living used to be more expensive.
    D   they agree that life used to be better.

33 How does Maude react to her husband?
    A   She resents his treatment of her.
    B   She thinks he can do no wrong.
    C   She finds his appearance embarrassing.
    D   She resists his suggestions.

34 What is Baden's attitude towards his wife?
    A   He admires her.
    B   He underestimates her.
    C   He is indulgent towards her.
    D   He dislikes her.

35 What is Simpkins' attitude towards Baden?
    A   critical disapproval
    B   secret admiration
    C   jealous rivalry
    D   amused tolerance

THIRD PASSAGE

On Tuesday I drove out to see my boat. I had firm ideas about what a boat
should be. One of the river books over which I'd pored during the summer
had been Henry Thoreau's *A Week on the Concord and Merrimack Rivers*.
Thoreau had made his inland voyage in a green and blue dory, 'a creature of
two elements, related by one half of its structure to some swift and shapely   5
fish, and by the other to some strong and graceful bird.' I had been tempted
to send this lovely specification on an airmail postcard to Crystal Marine.
    The boatyard lay far out of town, away from the river, at the end of a
dismal suburban boulevard. In the lot at the back, a hundred boats were
tipped up on trailers, identifiable only by their numbers. Mine was WS 1368   10
DD. It was just a mustard-coloured shell of aluminium. Blunt-backed, broad
in the beam, this bare piece of riveted metal did not look like a craft in which

one might float at all easily into a dream. It was related to neither fish nor
bird, but to some new efficient brand of non-stick saucepan.

Herb Heichert, the joint owner of the yard, stood by while I walked in a   15
slow circle round this unalluring object, trying to think of something polite
to say about it.

'Now we got to fix you up with the right rig for the river' he said. He
leaned on the transom. The boat boomed like a dull gong. Mr Heichert
pointed at the blank metallic space.   20

'All those hulls, they come in the same, and every one she goes out
different. You got to build it round the customer, right? No one's the same.
Everybody's different. That's America. That's the American Way. We're in
the customisation business here. You take a plain old hull and you build a
guy's whole identity into it. Look, I'll show you . . .'   25

He led me to his showroom. Boats hung on ropes from the ceiling, stood
on trailers and were rooted by their keels to the sides of the walls. My mind
boggled at the identities of the guys for whom they had been customised.
One was carpeted from bow to stern in blood-red synthetic fur, another in
the kind of artificial grass which undertakers spread over fresh graves.   30

'When a fella gets a boat he gets real sore if he sees some other fella
riding round the lake in a boat just like the one he's got himself. Round
here, everyone's an *individualist*.'

36   From this passage, we can guess that a dory (line 4) is a kind of
    A   plane.
    B   reptile.
    C   boat.
    D   carriage.

37   The author compares his boat to a non-stick saucepan in order to emphasise
    its
    A   colour.
    B   shape.
    C   size.
    D   ordinariness.

38   What is Mr Heichert's attitude towards his boats?
    A   pride
    B   embarrassment
    C   carelessness
    D   amazement

39   Which phrase draws attention to the American language?
    A   that's the American Way
    B   the guys for whom they had been customised
    C   blood-red synthetic fur
    D   everyone's an individualist

40 The words in the last paragraph are spoken by
   A   Mr Heichert in order to emphasise his point.
   B   Mr Heichert to make sure the author buys a boat.
   C   the author to make sure he gets a suitable boat.
   D   the author to make fun of Mr Heichert.

PAPER 2 COMPOSITION (2 hours)

*Write **two only** of the following composition exercises. Your answers must follow exactly the instructions given. Write in pen, not pencil. You are allowed to make alterations, but make sure that your work is clear and easy to read.*

1 Describe the kind of house or flat which would best suit your personality. (About 350 words)

2 'The purpose of television is to entertain, not to inform.' Discuss. (About 350 words)

3 Imagine that you have inherited £150,000. What would you do with it? (About 350 words)

4 The following letter appeared on the Problem Page of a popular magazine for women. Imagine you are Auntie Jo and write a suitable reply. (About 300 words)

> Dear Auntie Jo,
>
>   Three years ago I got married against the wishes of my parents. As it happened they were right and Bob left me last Autumn. Now Jason, my 11 month old son, and I are living with my parents. It was fine at first but now my mother seems to have taken against Jason and this has led to rows between her and my Dad and me. I don't know why she's like this or what to do. Please help!
>
>   Sincerely yours,
>
>

5   Basing your answer on your reading of the prescribed text concerned, answer **one** of the following. (About 350 words)

GEORGE ELIOT: *Silas Marner*
Explain the changing attitudes of the villagers of Raveloe towards Silas Marner.

PATRICIA HIGHSMITH: *The Talented Mr Ripley*
Why is Ripley called talented?

JOHN ARDEN: *Serjeant Musgrave's Dance*
What is Serjeant Musgrave's plan, and why does it fail?

PAPER 3   USE OF ENGLISH   (2 hours)

SECTION A

1   *Fill each of the numbered blanks in the following passage with* **one** *suitable word.*

Between about 9 months and perhaps 15 months infants become more diversified as human beings; they are now so clearly but variously affected .... (1) the environment in which they are .... (2) reared that it becomes increasingly difficult to categorize their development .... (3) to age. So for some people the term 'toddler' will apply .... (4) any infant under 3½; for .... (5) it will appear only to apply .... (6) to 20 months.

Being a toddler is a .... (7) like being an adolescent. The toddler is between babyhood and childhood, ... (8) as the adolescent is between childhood and adulthood. The .... (9) is often stereotyped as a rebel – as one .... (10) fights against the upbringing, the background, the restrictions he .... (11) accepted as a child; in the .... (12) way the toddler is often stereotyped as likely to .... (13) a problem to his parents. He too reaches a stage .... (14) he resents and fights the absolute power and control which his mother had .... (15) him when he was .... (16) baby. He too .... (17) for new fields in .... (18) to exercise a new sense of power, a new sense of self. But there the similarity has .... (19) its limits. Many adolescents are ready for self-determination; toddlers are .... (20).

2   *Finish each of the following sentences in such a way that it means exactly the same as the sentence printed before it.*

> EXAMPLE: Immediately after his arrival things went wrong.
> ANSWER: No sooner *had he arrived than things went wrong.*

a) The students regretted that they had missed the lecture.

The students regretted not ....

b) If you missed the programme you can't really judge.

Unless you ....

c) John and Mary moved to Edinburgh twenty years ago.

It is ....

d) She never seems to succeed, even though she works hard.

However ....

e) It was more of an argument than a discussion.

It was not so ....

f) I write to him almost every day.

Hardly ....

g) Mary told the police about the burglary.

Mary reported ....

h) I never intended to go to the meeting.

I never had ....

3   *Fill each of the blanks with a suitable word or phrase.*

> EXAMPLE: Even if I had stood on a chair, *I wouldn't have been able to*
> reach the light bulb.

a) On no occasion since then ....
against her mother's wishes.

b) You .... the prize or you'd
have heard by now.   ⟫▶

[97]

c) It's dark! Mind .... get lost!

d) He didn't take kindly ....
   criticised.

e) He likes nothing .... to sit
   and read the daily paper.

f) It must be twenty-five years ....
   at school.

4 *For each of the sentences below, write a new sentence* **as similar as possible in**
   meaning to the original sentence, *but using the word given. This word* **must not**
   be altered *in any way.*

   EXAMPLE: Not many people attended the meeting.
       turnout

   ANSWER: *There was a poor turnout for the meeting.*

   a) Dickens' last novel was unfinished when he died.
      without

      ....

   b) All the hostages were released yesterday by the kidnappers.
      let

      ....

   c) John was shocked to hear that he had failed his driving test.
      came

      ....

   d) He said he disapproved of people who smoked.
      expressed

      ....

   e) He is very likely to come.
      probability

      ....

f)   The cause of the explosion is still unknown.
     caused

....

g)   The judge sentenced the defendant to six months in prison.
     jailed

....

h)   I never thought of going by train.
     occurred

....

SECTION B

5   *Read the following passage, then answer the questions which follow it.*

The people of Marseille have a tendency to exaggerate, and you can't
spend long there without hearing the story about the sardine which
blocked the old harbour, the Vieux Port. In fact such an event really did
occur during the French Revolution, though the obstruction was caused
not by a fish of the herring family (for the Vieux Port is about 300 yards   5
wide) but by a ship called the Sardine which was placed there by
counter-revolutionaries blockading the insurgents. Or perhaps it was the
insurgents who were blockading the counter-revolutionaries: nowadays
most people have forgotten the origins of the story entirely, let alone the
details, and the sardine which blocked the Vieux Port now exists mainly   10
as a joking example of the Marseillais habit of presenting facts larger
than life-size.
     Almost as much as exaggeration, they like leg-pulling. I was there-
fore more than a little sceptical when the other day in Marseille I was told
that there was a whale on the beach. Initially I dismissed the story as a   15
piece of out-of-season April foolery.
     But there it was. When we arrived, the coastguards were winching it
up on to the jetty with steel hawsers wrapped around the tail. As it was
on its back you could easily see the deep folds along the front that
identified it as a Rorqual whale: Balenoptera Physalus, according to   20
Madame Turon of the Marseille Museum of Natural History.
     Being a whale it was, needless to say, enormous. It weighed 10 tons
and was 45 feet long. Even so, the poor thing was only a baby. Madame
Turon reckoned it was only a year old, for an adult grows to some 70
feet. She said it had died a natural death, probably as much as a month   25

[99]

ago, having somehow been separated from its school and succumbed to
thirst and hunger.

The body was scratched, presumably by having been washed up
against rocks, but at first sight seemed to be in a fairly good state. The
smell soon told you otherwise, and the temperature that day was well 30
up. It was an event that aroused a mixture of conflicting feelings.
Fascination and awe at the close-up spectacle of such a magnificent creature. Pity at the lack of dignity with which it was being hauled from its
element, backwards and upside down. Self-disgust at being part of the
crowd of gawping camera-clicking onlookers. 35

We left fairly soon, and were glad to have missed the sequel as
recorded in the next day's papers. The whale was being placed on the
back of a large lorry, its tail resting on the cabin, its head hanging off the
end. It was then driven to a factory to be cut up for its oils, highly valued
in the manufacture of cosmetics. Taking a corner of the Corniche 40
President John Kennedy, its decomposing tongue fell out on to the road.
It caused a traffic jam that was unusual even by the standards of Marseille, and one that will doubtless go down in legend along with the
sardine that blocked the Vieux Port.

a) In what way is the story told about the old harbour of Marseille exaggerated?

   ....

   ....

b) In what way was the story true? ....

   ....

c) Explain the meaning of the word 'insurgents' as used in line 7. ....

   ....

d) In the first paragraph, what is implied about the popular attitude to
   history?

   ....

   ....

e) What do the people of Marseille appear to believe about 'the story'
   (line 9) and why do they choose to believe this?

   ....

f) What reasons did the writer have for being sceptical about the existence of the whale?

....

....

g) Explain what is meant by the phrase 'out-of-season April foolery' (line 16).

....

h) What evidence did Madame Turon have to suggest that the whale was only a baby?

....

i) How was it suggested the whale had died? ....

....

j) How long had the whale been dead and what evidence was there of this?

....

k) In what way was the creature 'magnificent' (line 32)? ....

....

l) Explain in your own words the 'conflicting feelings' (line 31) of the writer.

....

....

m) What is a 'sequel' (line 36)? ....

....

n) What similarities are suggested in the last paragraph between the story of the sardine (line 2) and this story of the whale?

....

.... ⟫▶

o) In a short paragraph of 60–80 words, summarise everything we learn of this whale from its birth to its final end.

....

....

....

....

....

....

....

....

....

....

....

....

PAPER 4 LISTENING COMPREHENSION
(about 30 minutes)

FIRST PART

You will hear a conversation about keeping animals as pets.
For each of the questions 1 to 6 tick (✓) one box to show whether the statement is true or false.

	True	False
1 The woman is the dog's owner.		
2 The dog is very unfriendly.		
3 The dog has to stay outside.		
4 The woman would like a cat.		
5 The dog is too demanding.		
6 The woman thinks cats are more self-sufficient than dogs.		

SECOND PART

You will hear an extract from a radio programme in which Dr Knell interviews Gary Donan. For questions 7–11 tick (✓) one of the boxes A, B, C or D to show the correct answer.

7   At the beginning of the interview Dr Knell suggests that Gary is

A   ambitious.

B   extrovert.

C   withdrawn.

D   selfish.

A	
B	
C	
D	

8   Gary's sister Susan

A   encouraged him to take up acting.

B   acted with him on stage.

C   was once a professional dancer.

D   married a professional dancer.

A	
B	
C	
D	

9   How did his mother react to Gary's career?

A   favourably

B   critically

C   with surprise

D   with indifference

A	
B	
C	
D	

10   Gary and his father

A   got on well together.

B   quarrelled about acting.

C   held similar views.

D   disagreed about careers.

A	
B	
C	
D	

11 Gary's father hoped his son would

   A   achieve more than he had himself.

   B   become a successful banker.

   C   follow the same pattern as he had.

   D   attend the same university.

A	
B	
C	
D	

THIRD PART

You will hear a recorded telephone announcement about visiting Edinburgh in Scotland.
For questions 12–21 fill in the gaps below.

SPEND A DAY OUT IN EDINBURGH

Open to the public: Cannongate Tollbooth Museum

Exhibition of original (12) ....

Open: (13) .... to 6 p.m.

Coach Tours: depart from Waverley (14) ....

tel: (15) ....

Join the Scottish Tours Guides for a conducted excursion along the (16) ....

Edinburgh Zoo: contains over (17) .... different species

only (18) .... minutes from the city centre

Buses 12
      26
(19) ....
      86

Princes St. Gardens: Ross open air (20) ....

Programme begins at 3 p.m.

7.30 Alistair Wood and his Scottish (21) .... dance band.

FOURTH PART

You will hear a man discussing the difficulties of managing a printing studio.
For questions 22–28 tick (✓) one of the boxes A, B, C or D to show the correct answer.

22 Why did he regularly delegate responsibility?

    A He disliked the work.

    B He was running the studio.

    C He had too many people to organise.

    D He was extremely busy.

A	
B	
C	
D	

23 How was he feeling when he wrote the words for Barry?

    A furious

    B resigned

    C nervous

    D distressed

A	
B	
C	
D	

24 How did Barry react when Jan pointed out the mistake?

    A He wanted to change it.

    B He wanted to check it with Abbas.

    C He didn't believe Jan.

    D He refused to do anything.

A	
B	
C	
D	

25 When did the production manager discover the error?

    A during typesetting

    B during the colour printing

    C when the leaflets were ready to send off

    D when the leaflets had been delivered to the customer

A	
B	
C	
D	

26 How did Barry feel about Abbas?

A He got on all right with him.

B They were close friends.

C He disliked him intensely.

D He resented his impersonal manner.

A	
B	
C	
D	

27 What was Barry's attitude to the firm?

A He was actively hostile.

B He didn't understand the responsibilities.

C He was only loyal to his own department.

D He wanted to make the managers look foolish.

A	
B	
C	
D	

28 What result of poor management is being discussed?

A badly-trained staff

B overworked managers

C disloyal employees

D argumentative workers

A	
B	
C	
D	

PAPER 5   INTERVIEW   (15–20 minutes)

You will be asked to take part in a conversation with a group of other students or with your teacher. The conversation will be based on one particular topic area or theme, for example holidays, work, food.

Of course each interview will be different for each student or group of students, but a *typical* interview is described below.

* At the start of the interview you will be asked to talk about one of the photographs among the Interview Exercises at the back of the book.

* You will then be asked to discuss one of the passages at the back of the book. Your teacher may ask you to talk about its content, where you think it comes from, who the author or speaker is, whether you agree or disagree with it, and so on. You will *not* be asked to read the passage aloud, but you may quote parts of it to make your point.

* You may then be asked to discuss for example an advertisement, a leaflet, extract from a newspaper etc. Your teacher will tell you which of the Interview Exercises to look at.

* You may also be asked to take part in an activity with a group of other students or your teacher. Your teacher will tell you which section among the Interview Exercises you should look at.

Interview Exercises

CULTURE

1

2   Taking the trouble to X-ray Manet's work may, at first, seem absurd. Why bother to probe beneath the surface of paintings which look so candid, spontaneous and decisively organised? What chance would there be of discovering dramatic changes by an artist who always appears so free of agonising doubt? As for building an entire exhibition around the results of a comprehensive X-ray examination of his key canvasses, the notion sounds frankly eccentric.

3   Both the week's other movies, *Miracles* (Cannon, Panton Street, PG) and *Jake speed* (Cannon, Haymarket, 15) are the sort of thing you only normally come across on the shelves of your local video shop. Why this particular pair should have been thought worthy of promoting in cinemas is hard to say. They are so bad that one cannot imagine how anyone of sound mind would have invested a dollar, let alone six or seven million, in either.

4 She took up drums after instantly copying percussion patterns which a woman demonstrator at a local youth centre told her had taken months to learn. She was also a star of local brass bands while a student. 'The music department was so proud of me it used to use me as an example to the boys. I don't agree with all that now – you know 'If a girl can do it, why can't you?' – but it gave me a lot of confidence at the time.

5

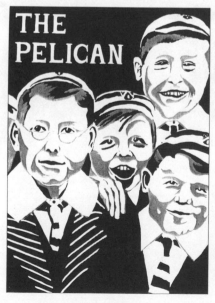

6 The examiner will ask you to imagine the following situation:

Due to a lengthy strike, or other long-term breakdown, there will be no television in your country for several months.

You will be asked to estimate the effect of this TV blackout
a) on your own way of life;
b) on the society you live in.

ADVERTISING

7

8   Considerations of how the nature of the product or service will influence the nature of the message.

Can it be treated humorously or seriously? Should the emphasis be on lengthy, technical explanation of the product in operation? Is visual treatment important? Is the product of service best portrayed in an atmosphere of escapism or romance? What is known about why users buy this category of product or service and how will this influence the nature of the message?

9   Supermom stayed home and when the kiddies came back from school she baked them cookies in the shape of pumpkins with raisin eyes and carrot noses. But now we have before us the ideal of Superwoman who prepares a well-balanced nutritious breakfast for her children, and her children eat it. She goes off to work where she makes $30,000 a year as an executive of a law firm. She comes home and reads to the children, then serves dinner by candlelight to her husband.

10   Nature has the answer for blocked-up stuffy noses. Natural Olbas Oil. Just a few drops of natural Olbas Oil on a tissue or handkerchief, and a deep breathe-in gives immediate relief. For catarrh, colds, sinus and nasal congestion.

Olbas Oil is the unique blend of 6 natural pure plant oils and menthol Cajuput, cloves, eucalyptus, peppermint, wintergreen, and juniper berries. For all the family, including the children.

11

Learn to speak a new language.
Anytime! Anywhere!

Speak French, German or Spanish with ease in 30-45 hours – *or all your money back!*

How would you like to speak another language? Of course you would. Haven't the time? If you've time to drive a car ... or have a bath, you've time to learn a second language. How? With the Language Courses from Reader's Digest. Just pop on a cassette whenever you have some spare moments, then listen and repeat. You have no boring textbooks to read ... no complicated grammar to learn. Think how much time you waste in traffic jams. You could be using that time to learn another language.

So don't waste any more time: fill in the coupon and send for your free cassette and brochure right away.

Learn in your spare moments

FREE ◀◀
DEMONSTRATION CASSETTE

Send now for your demonstration cassette and start learning right away. There's absolutely no obligation.

SPEAK FRENCH IN ONLY 3 MONTHS! (or German, Spanish, Italian, Dutch, Swedish, Portuguese or Greek)

Radio Times readers now have an opportunity to buy the world-famous Hugo Cassette Course for **ONLY £25.95** – a saving of £5.00 on the normal price – **plus a free pocket dictionary.**
At this special price it is an unbeatable investment for business or pleasure, for yourself, your company, or your family. You could pay a lot more for a language course of such high quality. With Hugo there is no risk; you may listen to the course for two weeks at home and return it for a full refund of your money if you are not absolutely satisfied.

*SPECIAL OFFER £5 SAVING!
AND
FREE! WITH EVERY ORDER...
POCKET DICTIONARY
(This offer closes on 16.3.87)

WHICH OF THESE LANGUAGES WOULD YOU LIKE TO SPEAK?

Tick the one you want to speak in 3 months' time...

☐ Afrikaans	☐ Finnish	☐ Indonesian	☐ Portuguese
☐ American English	☐ French	☐ Irish	☐ Russian
☐ Arabic (Modern)	☐ German	☐ Italian	☐ Serbo-Croat
☐ Chinese (Mandarin)	Greek (Modern)	☐ Japanese	☐ Spanish (Castilian)
☐ Danish	☐ Hebrew (Modern)	☐ Korean	☐ Spanish (Latin American)
☐ Dutch	☐ Hindi	☐ Malay	☐ Swedish
☐ English	☐ Icelandic	☐ Norwegian	☐ Thai
		☐ Polish	☐ Welsh

It's really a lot easier and faster than you'd expect when you learn the Linguaphone way. You simply learn at your own pace, as and when it suits you best. And you'll be following a course prepared by some of the world's leading language experts. You'll get the accent right, too. With Linguaphone, all it takes is as little as half an hour a day and you could be speaking a new language in 3 months from now.

For your FREE DEMONSTRATION PACK containing cassette, course booklet and full-colour brochure, simply complete and post the coupon now.

FREE OFFER

Free! This personal stereo cassette player is yours free when you order your Linguaphone language course.

12 The examiner will ask you to imagine that you are part of an advertising team working to promote a new kind of soft drink. Consider the guidelines below, and discuss and decide how and where you should market your new product to achieve the best results.

Advertising guidelines
– What market are we aiming at?
– What kind of image do we want to project?
– What type of attitude shall we adopt – amusing, serious, sexy, scientific etc.?
– What will be the most effective places to advertise our product – television, magazines, newspapers, cinema, street posters etc.?

EMERGENCIES

13

14   After the first week they stopped saying they hoped it would not rain and began to take precautions against fire.

Grass and bracken were tinder-dry and there had been one or two fires in thatched cottages. On the beaches the sand was blistering to the feet and midday saw only the hardiest of sun-worshippers exposing their bodies. Dustbins and drains were smelling. Milk had turned sour before it was taken from the doorstep. Cases of sunstroke vied with sufferers from sickness and diarrhoea in doctors' surgeries. In the evenings, the air was choked with exhaust fumes as the cars queued to get off the island.

15   A man was critically ill in hospital yesterday after a fire at a chemical plant on Sunday during which toxic gas was released. He was one of three workers in the intensive care unit of the North Tees General Hospital after the incident in which a fertiliser dryer overheated, causing fumes to drift over the St Hilda's area of Middlesbrough. A company spokesman said the cloud was essentially nitrous oxide with traces of hydrochloric acid and ammonia.

[117]

16 There were two youngsters standing near me about five or six years old. One of them was bleeding because his face had been cut. I think their father was lying near them. I think he was dead. I helped the little ones climb over the barrier and that was all I could do. Then I fought my way to the front and climbed out myself. It was terrible.

17

Defective heaters danger warning

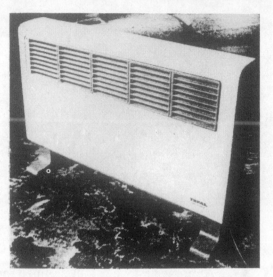

HOUSEHOLDERS should still be aware of some Tefal convector heaters which have been recalled because of a possible wiring defect.

This newspaper warned about the heaters following a statement by Barnet Trading Standards Office before Christmas.

But at least one couple in the borough, who were given a Tefal heater by Barnet Council, used it over Christmas, unaware of the possible danger.

Models 64.47, 64.41, and 64.43 similar to that pictured here should be taken to a Tefal Service Centre for a free adjustment.

The addresses of the Service Centres are available by ringing the Teledata service on 200–0200.

18 The examiner will ask you to give your views on the following: 'The media are too concerned with disasters. More attention should be paid to less sensational news items'.

ANIMAL WELFARE

19

20   White-tailed sea eagles have bred successfully in Scotland for the second year running according to the Royal Society for the Protection of Birds. Under the Sea Eagle Project, a pair, which bred last year, have successfully raised two chicks. The birds, which first attempted to breed in 1983, have been guarded round the clock by wardens at a secret nest site.

21   DRIVE OR WALK AROUND
Come and roam around Britain's greatest open zoo. Take a train across the 'Asian Plains' and wander round the 'African Veld'. You'll see some of the world's rarest animals, from majestic tigers to the near-extinct Przewalski's wild horses. Look out for the famous herd of white rhinos. Be sure to see the cheetahs which have bred so well.

22   During the summer a profusion of wild plants produce seed which is the winter food for the ducks and swans which are attracted to the marshy ground. Usually there is sufficiently deep water for diving ducks such as pochard, while large areas which are scarcely covered by water are favoured by enormous flocks of birds such as teal and mallard. Swans swim majestically on the wide areas of shallow lakes, while plovers and waders find food on the high land and near the waters' edge.

23 LONDON ZOO
Everybody's zooing it!

SO MUCH TO DO . . .

More than 8,000 animals live at London Zoo. Bongos, bush-babies, bats and boas – come for a day and meet them all. Get nose-to-nose with a tiger. See the giant panda munching bamboo. Walk with a baby elephant. Chat with a mynah. Call in on the scorpions. Look at the night prowlers in the Moonlight World.

On fine days from Easter to the end of September, ride a camel, pony or donkey; take a spin in the pony or llama traps. Join the elephants' weighing and bath time. Meet the animals at their afternoon show.

There are cafés, a restaurant, kiosks and bars for lunches, teas and in-between snacks – souvenirs and films from the Zoo Shop – pushchairs and wheelchairs for hire.

. . . MORE THAN JUST A DAY OUT

FEEDING TIMES

All year, enjoy the animal feeding times – Pelicans and Penguins every afternoon, and Sealions every afternoon but Fridays (when their pond is cleaned). And there's a special feed on Fridays only for the snakes, alligators and lizards in the Reptile House.

OTHER EVENTS All year through, the cows are milked at 3 pm in Children's Zoo. And from Easter to September, there's all the fun of the elephants' weighing and bathtime, and the chance to meet some of the baby animals and their keepers at the 'Meet the Animals' show each afternoon.

OPENING HOURS

London Zoo is open every day of the year except Christmas Day.

24 The examiner will ask you to speak either for or against the following motion: 'It is folly to concern ourselves with the welfare of animals while our fellow human beings need our help.' You may like to think about the following points when preparing your speech:
– animals are sentient creatures like humans
– man cannot survive without animals
– what legacy we leave to future generations
– exploitation of animals for benefit of humans (e.g. medical research)
– resources devoted to animals not available for human victims of hardship

[121]

MONARCHY

25

26 The bride of the year, Miss Sarah Ferguson, entered Westminster Abbey yesterday a commoner, a girl from the shires in a headdress of summer flowers, and emerged glittering with diamonds as Her Royal Highness, The Duchess of York, wife of Prince Andrew, the newly-created Duke of York.

27 BOOK SIX Which treats of the life, works, and conquests of the Inca Pachacutec, ninth king of Peru. With a description of the royal mansions; of the funeral ceremonies of the kings; of the hunting season; posts and messengers; Empire archives and accounts.

28

PHILADELPHIA / NEW YORK
This morning visit Philadelphia, the home of the First and Second
Continental Congresses and first capital of the U.S. Enjoy a brief
sightseeing tour of the city before arriving at Independence Hall, site
of the signing of the Declaration of Independence and home of the
Liberty Bell.

29

*Plan of the Chamber of the House
of Lords showing the Woolsack and
the positions of the Government,
Opposition and Cross Benches*

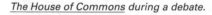

The House of Commons during a debate.

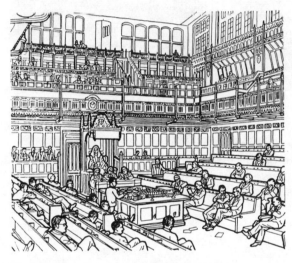

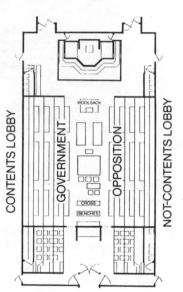

30

a) What are the biggest changes you would make if you were in
charge of the government of your country / of Britain?

b) What do you see as the most difficult problems facing the
government in your country / in Britain?

OPTIONAL READING

Patricia Highsmith: *The Talented Mr Ripley*

31

32 Tom had never seen them, but he could see them now, precise draughtsman's drawings with every line and bolt and screw labelled, could see Dickie smiling, holding them up for him to look at and he could have gone on for several minutes describing details for Mr Greenleaf's delight, but he checked himself.

33 He chose a dark-blue silk tie and knotted it carefully. The suit fitted him. He re-parted his hair and put the parting a little more to one side, the way Dickie wore his.
'Marge, you must understand that I don't *love* you,' Tom said into the mirror in Dickie's voice, with Dickie's higher pitch on the emphasised words.

34 He hated Dickie, because, however he looked at what had happened, his failing had not been his own fault, not due to anything he had done, but due to Dickie's inhuman stubbornness. And his blatant rudeness. He had offered Dickie friendship, companionship and respect, everything he had to offer and Dickie had replied with ingratitude and now hostility.

35 The examiner will ask you to discuss one or more of the following topics:

1 How much does the chief character manipulate the plot?
2 the situation of any one or more characters, in a 'What could he/she have done?' context.
3 reasons for liking or disliking the book.
4 insights into the society and attitudes portrayed.
5 the setting and descriptive background.
6 Could this novel be called a study in madness?
7 What is our attitude to Ripley? Do we want the police to catch up with him?
8 Would this novel make a good film?

Acknowledgements

The University of Cambridge Local Examinations Syndicate and the publishers are grateful to the following for permission to reproduce texts and illustrations. It has not been possible to identify sources of all the material used and in such cases the publishers would welcome information from copyright owners.

Basil Blackwell Ltd. for the extract from *The Micro Electronics Revolution* by Tom Forester on pp. 7–8; Hamish Hamilton for the extract from *Strange Meeting* by Susan Hill on p. 47; Weidenfeld and Nicolson Ltd for the extract from *Landscape – National Trust Book of Long Walks* by Adam Nicolson on p. 48; Mitchell Beazley Publishers for the extract from the *International Book of Wood* on pp. 65–6; The Literary Executors of Vera Brittain for the extract on p. 67 from *Testament of Friendship* published by Virago Press; The Guardian for the extract on pp. 68–9; William Collins Sons and Co. Ltd. and Aitken and Stone Ltd. for the extract from *Old Glory* by Jonathan Raban on pp. 91–2; Penguin Books Ltd for the cover illustration on p. 125 from *The Talented Mr Ripley* by Patricia Highsmith. The extract on pp. 4–5 is reprinted by permission of Faber and Faber Ltd from *The Skull Beneath the Skin* by P. D. James.

All other texts, illustrations and photographs were supplied by the University of Cambridge Local Examinations Syndicate.

H

OBJECTIVE TEST ANSWER SHEET

Subject/Paper No.

Subject Name

Centre/Candidate Number..

Candidate Name..

} If your Centre/Candidate Number
and Name are not shown, please
enter them on the dotted lines.

A. GENERAL INSTRUCTIONS TO THE CANDIDATE

1. TELL THE SUPERVISOR IMMEDIATELY IF YOUR CENTRE/CANDIDATE NUMBER OR NAME ARE INCORRECT.

2. IF THE INFORMATION ABOVE IS CORRECT, PLEASE SIGN HERE. ....

3. USE A SOFT HB PENCIL ONLY FOR YOUR ANSWERS ON THIS SHEET.
   DO NOT USE INK OR BALL POINT PEN.

B. INSTRUCTIONS FOR RECORDING ANSWERS

1. SUGGESTED ANSWERS TO EACH QUESTION ARE GIVEN IN THE QUESTION PAPER, CHOOSE AN ANSWER AND SHADE THE SPACE BELOW THE CORRESPONDING LETTER ON THIS SHEET THUS ▬

2. ERRORS — THOROUGHLY RUB OUT ANY ERRORS WITH A CLEAN RUBBER. LEAVE NO SMUDGES.

	A	B	C	D			A	B	C	D
1	▭	▭	▭	▭		21	▭	▭	▭	▭
2	▭	▭	▭	▭		22	▭	▭	▭	▭
3	▭	▭	▭	▭		23	▭	▭	▭	▭
4	▭	▭	▭	▭		24	▭	▭	▭	▭
5	▭	▭	▭	▭		25	▭	▭	▭	▭
6	▭	▭	▭	▭		26	▭	▭	▭	▭
7	▭	▭	▭	▭		27	▭	▭	▭	▭
8	▭	▭	▭	▭		28	▭	▭	▭	▭
9	▭	▭	▭	▭		29	▭	▭	▭	▭
10	▭	▭	▭	▭		30	▭	▭	▭	▭
11	▭	▭	▭	▭		31	▭	▭	▭	▭
12	▭	▭	▭	▭		32	▭	▭	▭	▭
13	▭	▭	▭	▭		33	▭	▭	▭	▭
14	▭	▭	▭	▭		34	▭	▭	▭	▭
15	▭	▭	▭	▭		35	▭	▭	▭	▭
16	▭	▭	▭	▭		36	▭	▭	▭	▭
17	▭	▭	▭	▭		37	▭	▭	▭	▭
18	▭	▭	▭	▭		38	▭	▭	▭	▭
19	▭	▭	▭	▭		39	▭	▭	▭	▭
20	▭	▭	▭	▭		40	▭	▭	▭	▭

H

OBJECTIVE TEST ANSWER SHEET

Subject/Paper No.
Subject Name

Centre/Candidate Number..

Candidate Name...

} If your Centre/Candidate Number
and Name are not shown, please
enter them on the dotted lines.

A. GENERAL INSTRUCTIONS TO THE CANDIDATE

1. TELL THE SUPERVISOR IMMEDIATELY IF YOUR CENTRE/CANDIDATE NUMBER OR NAME ARE INCORRECT.

2. IF THE INFORMATION ABOVE IS CORRECT, PLEASE SIGN HERE. ....

3. USE A SOFT HB PENCIL ONLY FOR YOUR ANSWERS ON THIS SHEET.
   DO NOT USE INK OR BALL POINT PEN.

B. INSTRUCTIONS FOR RECORDING ANSWERS

1. SUGGESTED ANSWERS TO EACH QUESTION ARE GIVEN IN THE QUESTION PAPER. CHOOSE AN ANSWER
   AND SHADE THE SPACE BELOW THE CORRESPONDING LETTER ON THIS SHEET THUS 𝐀

2. ERRORS — THOROUGHLY RUB OUT ANY ERRORS WITH A CLEAN RUBBER. LEAVE NO SMUDGES.

	A	B	C	D			A	B	C	D
1	⊂⊃	⊂⊃	⊂⊃	⊂⊃		21	⊂⊃	⊂⊃	⊂⊃	⊂⊃
2	⊂⊃	⊂⊃	⊂⊃	⊂⊃		22	⊂⊃	⊂⊃	⊂⊃	⊂⊃
3	⊂⊃	⊂⊃	⊂⊃	⊂⊃		23	⊂⊃	⊂⊃	⊂⊃	⊂⊃
4	⊂⊃	⊂⊃	⊂⊃	⊂⊃		24	⊂⊃	⊂⊃	⊂⊃	⊂⊃
5	⊂⊃	⊂⊃	⊂⊃	⊂⊃		25	⊂⊃	⊂⊃	⊂⊃	⊂⊃
6	⊂⊃	⊂⊃	⊂⊃	⊂⊃		26	⊂⊃	⊂⊃	⊂⊃	⊂⊃
7	⊂⊃	⊂⊃	⊂⊃	⊂⊃		27	⊂⊃	⊂⊃	⊂⊃	⊂⊃
8	⊂⊃	⊂⊃	⊂⊃	⊂⊃		28	⊂⊃	⊂⊃	⊂⊃	⊂⊃
9	⊂⊃	⊂⊃	⊂⊃	⊂⊃		29	⊂⊃	⊂⊃	⊂⊃	⊂⊃
10	⊂⊃	⊂⊃	⊂⊃	⊂⊃		30	⊂⊃	⊂⊃	⊂⊃	⊂⊃
11	⊂⊃	⊂⊃	⊂⊃	⊂⊃		31	⊂⊃	⊂⊃	⊂⊃	⊂⊃
12	⊂⊃	⊂⊃	⊂⊃	⊂⊃		32	⊂⊃	⊂⊃	⊂⊃	⊂⊃
13	⊂⊃	⊂⊃	⊂⊃	⊂⊃		33	⊂⊃	⊂⊃	⊂⊃	⊂⊃
14	⊂⊃	⊂⊃	⊂⊃	⊂⊃		34	⊂⊃	⊂⊃	⊂⊃	⊂⊃
15	⊂⊃	⊂⊃	⊂⊃	⊂⊃		35	⊂⊃	⊂⊃	⊂⊃	⊂⊃
16	⊂⊃	⊂⊃	⊂⊃	⊂⊃		36	⊂⊃	⊂⊃	⊂⊃	⊂⊃
17	⊂⊃	⊂⊃	⊂⊃	⊂⊃		37	⊂⊃	⊂⊃	⊂⊃	⊂⊃
18	⊂⊃	⊂⊃	⊂⊃	⊂⊃		38	⊂⊃	⊂⊃	⊂⊃	⊂⊃
19	⊂⊃	⊂⊃	⊂⊃	⊂⊃		39	⊂⊃	⊂⊃	⊂⊃	⊂⊃
20	⊂⊃	⊂⊃	⊂⊃	⊂⊃		40	⊂⊃	⊂⊃	⊂⊃	⊂⊃

H

OBJECTIVE TEST ANSWER SHEET

Subject/Paper No.
Subject Name

Centre/Candidate Number...

Candidate Name..

} If your Centre/Candidate Number
and Name are not shown, please
enter them on the dotted lines.

A. GENERAL INSTRUCTIONS TO THE CANDIDATE

1. TELL THE SUPERVISOR IMMEDIATELY IF YOUR CENTRE/CANDIDATE NUMBER OR NAME ARE INCORRECT.

2. IF THE INFORMATION ABOVE IS CORRECT, PLEASE SIGN HERE. ....

3. USE A SOFT HB PENCIL ONLY FOR YOUR ANSWERS ON THIS SHEET.
   DO NOT USE INK OR BALL POINT PEN.

B. INSTRUCTIONS FOR RECORDING ANSWERS

1. SUGGESTED ANSWERS TO EACH QUESTION ARE GIVEN IN THE QUESTION PAPER, CHOOSE AN ANSWER
   AND SHADE THE SPACE BELOW THE CORRESPONDING LETTER ON THIS SHEET THUS ▪A▪

2. ERRORS — THOROUGHLY RUB OUT ANY ERRORS WITH A CLEAN RUBBER. LEAVE NO SMUDGES.

	A	B	C	D			A	B	C	D
1	⊂⊃	⊂⊃	⊂⊃	⊂⊃	21	⊂⊃	⊂⊃	⊂⊃	⊂⊃
2	⊂⊃	⊂⊃	⊂⊃	⊂⊃	22	⊂⊃	⊂⊃	⊂⊃	⊂⊃
3	⊂⊃	⊂⊃	⊂⊃	⊂⊃	23	⊂⊃	⊂⊃	⊂⊃	⊂⊃
4	⊂⊃	⊂⊃	⊂⊃	⊂⊃	24	⊂⊃	⊂⊃	⊂⊃	⊂⊃
5	⊂⊃	⊂⊃	⊂⊃	⊂⊃	25	⊂⊃	⊂⊃	⊂⊃	⊂⊃
6	⊂⊃	⊂⊃	⊂⊃	⊂⊃	26	⊂⊃	⊂⊃	⊂⊃	⊂⊃
7	⊂⊃	⊂⊃	⊂⊃	⊂⊃	27	⊂⊃	⊂⊃	⊂⊃	⊂⊃
8	⊂⊃	⊂⊃	⊂⊃	⊂⊃	28	⊂⊃	⊂⊃	⊂⊃	⊂⊃
9	⊂⊃	⊂⊃	⊂⊃	⊂⊃	29	⊂⊃	⊂⊃	⊂⊃	⊂⊃
10	⊂⊃	⊂⊃	⊂⊃	⊂⊃	30	⊂⊃	⊂⊃	⊂⊃	⊂⊃
11	⊂⊃	⊂⊃	⊂⊃	⊂⊃	31	⊂⊃	⊂⊃	⊂⊃	⊂⊃
12	⊂⊃	⊂⊃	⊂⊃	⊂⊃	32	⊂⊃	⊂⊃	⊂⊃	⊂⊃
13	⊂⊃	⊂⊃	⊂⊃	⊂⊃	33	⊂⊃	⊂⊃	⊂⊃	⊂⊃
14	⊂⊃	⊂⊃	⊂⊃	⊂⊃	34	⊂⊃	⊂⊃	⊂⊃	⊂⊃
15	⊂⊃	⊂⊃	⊂⊃	⊂⊃	35	⊂⊃	⊂⊃	⊂⊃	⊂⊃
16	⊂⊃	⊂⊃	⊂⊃	⊂⊃	36	⊂⊃	⊂⊃	⊂⊃	⊂⊃
17	⊂⊃	⊂⊃	⊂⊃	⊂⊃	37	⊂⊃	⊂⊃	⊂⊃	⊂⊃
18	⊂⊃	⊂⊃	⊂⊃	⊂⊃	38	⊂⊃	⊂⊃	⊂⊃	⊂⊃
19	⊂⊃	⊂⊃	⊂⊃	⊂⊃	39	⊂⊃	⊂⊃	⊂⊃	⊂⊃
20	⊂⊃	⊂⊃	⊂⊃	⊂⊃	40	⊂⊃	⊂⊃	⊂⊃	⊂⊃